MW00441206

Twelve Facets of Reality

OTHER BOOKS BY GURUDEV SHREE CHITRABHANU

Lotus Bloom
Fountain of Inspiration
Inspiring Anecdotes
Bondage and Freedom
The Beacon
Jain Master Speaks to One World
Ten Days Journey into the Self
Sense Beyond the Senses
The Philosophy of Soul and Matter
Realize What You Are: The Dynamics of Jain Meditation
The Psychology of Enlightenment: Meditations on the Seven Energy Centers

TWELVE FACETS

The Jain Pat

NEW YOR

OF REALITY

to Freedom

by Gurudev Shree Chitrabhanu

Edited by Clare Rosenfield

DODD, MEAD & COMPANY

Jain Meditation International Center
120 East 86 Street
New York, N.Y.
Tel: 212-722-7474

Printed in the United States of America

1 2 3 4 5 6 7 8 9 10

Library of Congress Cataloging in Publication Data

Chandraprabhsagar, Muni, 1922–
Twelve facets of reality.

1. Jaina meditations. 2. Spiritual life
(Jainism)—Collected works. I. Rosenfield, Clare.
II. Title.
BL1378.7.C6 294.4'44 80-16773
ISBN 0-396-07902-4

To My Immortal Father

Pujya Munishree Chandrakant Sagarji

Whatever blooms have
blossomed forth are all from
the seeds you planted

Contents

The Immortal Song

May the sacred stream of amity flow forever in my heart,
May the universe prosper, such is my cherished desire;
May my heart sing with ecstasy at the sight of the virtuous,
And may my life be an offering at their feet;
May my heart bleed at the sight of the wretched, the cruel, and the poor,
And may tears of compassion flow from my eyes;
May I always be there to show the path to the pathless wanderers of life,
Yet if they should not hearken to me, may I bide patiently;
May the spirit of goodwill enter into all our hearts,
May we all sing together the immortal song of brotherhood,
The immortal song of sisterhood,
The immortal song.

—*Shree Chitrabhanu*

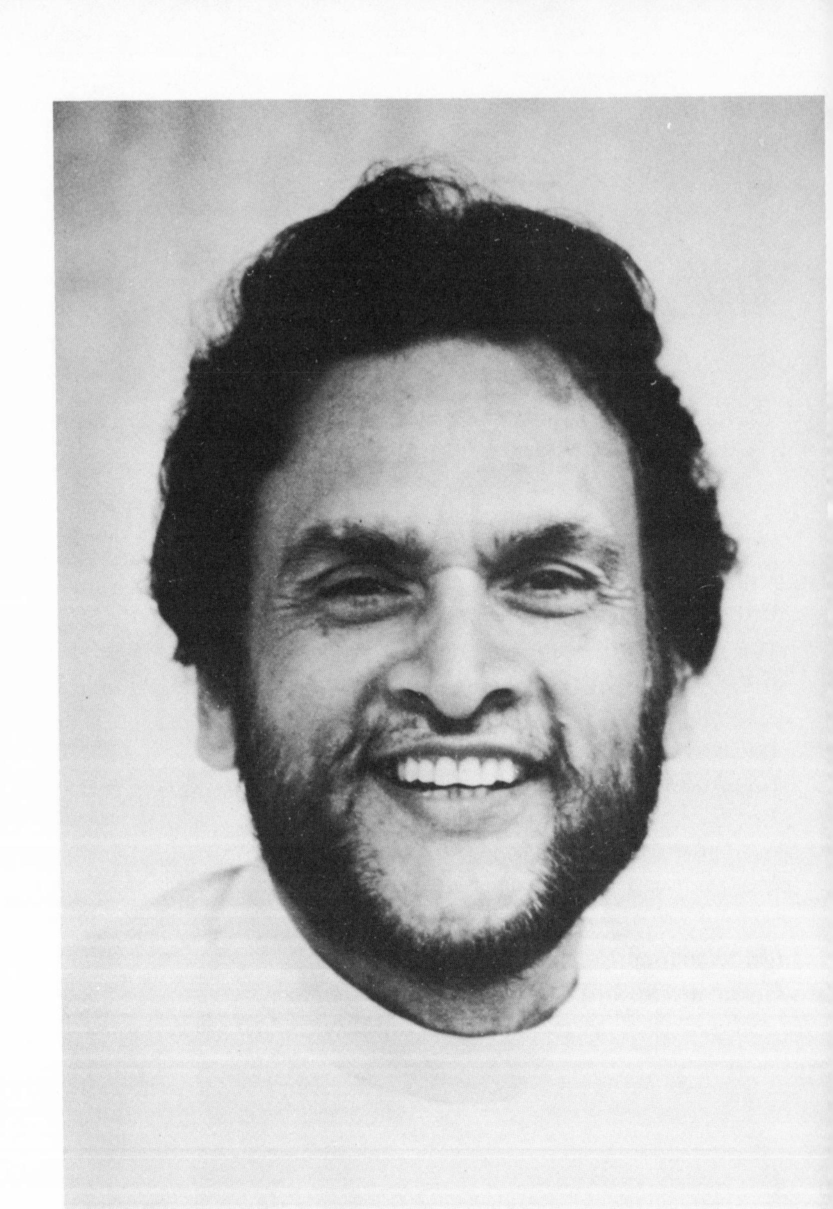

Introduction

"JUST as a mighty mango tree is hidden within the stone of the mango, even so, O man, divinity itself is hidden within you. Rest not until you uncover it."

These words, spoken more than twenty-five hundred years ago by the twenty-fourth Prophet of Jainism, Bhagwan Mahavir, resounded in the heart of Gurudev Shree Chitrabhanu when he first heard them as a young adult. This seed-thought continued to grow, blossom, and bear fruit throughout his life's experiences. Before he became a monk at the age of twenty he was inspired by two shining examples of the divine in man: his loving and highly principled father, and Mahatma Gandhi, with whom he worked for the freedom of India.

Events in his life accelerated the process of his inner ripening. At four years of age, he lost his mother, and at eleven his younger sister. As a college student, he won a severe bout with rheumatic fever, during which time he glimpsed his soul's longing to live in light and service to all. In his second year of working in Gandhiji's non-cooperation movement, he lost his closest and dearest friend. Then he lost his peace. He confronted and unmasked questions which lay smoldering in his consciousness: "Is there some meaning to life? Do we have some mission, or are we to pass the years only in filling and emptying the body, in collecting and rearranging things? Where did my loved ones go? What is the point of living if those dearest to us depart from us sooner or later?"

Rather than give in to the pain, depression, and confusion of those moments, he took a positive step. In search of permanent understanding, he discovered a genuine master who initiated him into the Jain monkhood and advised him: "Books and other people's answers alone cannot illumine you. You have to dive into yourself. Why do you not have the experience of your own life?"

Through patience, introspection, and the practice of silence for the greater part of five years, he began to remove the clouds of his unawareness. Living the itinerant life of a monk in the inspiring company of his master as well as his revered father, who became a monk along with him, he came closer and closer to his own reality. One night he unlocked the door which had sealed him from the knowledge of Self. He experienced fully the radiant sunlight of his being.

From that moment, his life became an actualization of his inner reality. It was his inborn gift to be able to melt the hearts of listeners and readers by his vibrant, poignant, and direct words arising from his own experience. In twenty-nine years as a monk, he walked barefoot over thirty thousand miles bringing people out from their pettiness, sectarianism, and closed-mindedness into the realm of the highest and noblest in them. As people's hearts were touched, they began to transform their lives. They attuned themselves to Mahavir's universal message and took the ideal of reverence for all life into the practical details of their day-to-day living.

In Bombay, Gurudev turned his energies to the stream of social action. He founded the Divine Knowledge Society, to which his students offered complete dedication. When a natural disaster, famine, or flood struck, teams of volunteers would go to those areas and distribute food, clothing, blankets, and medicines. The words of Mahavir came to life in the numerous instances of their giving of themselves: "Since you receive more than any other form of life, it is natural that you will want to give more."

Gurudev soon became one of the well-known spiritual leaders of the Jains in India. Founders of the Temple of Understanding invited him to address their First, Second, and Third Spiritual Summit Conferences in Calcutta and Geneva and at the Harvard Divinity School in 1968, 1970, and 1971, respectively. Gurudev's decision to attend in person the last two conferences represented a daring step. It was the first time in five thousand years of known Jain history that a Jain monk had traveled outside of India. The winds of change were stirring within him. He rejected precedent, tradition, and public opinion, and risked his position of great authority and respect in order to bring the universal teaching of reverence for life to the larger human family.

Inspired by the genuineness of his message, Gurudev's audiences in Europe, Africa, and America urged him to stay and teach them. Moved by their sincerity and eagerness to learn, Gurudev gave up the orthodox life of a monk, his title and post, and accepted the many invitations to teach in America. Among the institutions of human development sponsoring his talks were the United Nations, Koinonia Foundation, Pendle Hill, Wainwright House, Princeton, Sarah Lawrence, Cornell, the State University of New York at Purchase, and many others. He became for a time president of the World Fellowship of Religions, and worked closely with individuals involved in the Temple of Understanding and in the fields of yoga, psychiatry, philosophy, and government.

Founder of the Jain Meditation International Center in New York City, of which Gurudev is the spiritual leader, he has inspired his students in Brazil, India, Canada, Kenya, England, and diverse parts of America to open centers where the philosophy of reverence for life can be taught and practiced. Throughout the many changing phases of his life, as a monk or a family man, as a teacher or a student, he has been communicating from his heart the underlying oneness he feels with all forms of life, inviting mankind to see, experience, and rejoice.

—Clare Rosenfield

Preface

IN this universe, all of us are on different levels of seeing, of understanding, of experiencing. Some of us are caught by the bramble bushes at the foot of the mountain. Others are halfway to the summit, but because of clouded vision, take two steps backward for every two steps forward and reach nowhere. Still others are hurtling their way downward, unable to keep their footing, unable to glimpse their purpose. Those human beings who consistently and carefully remove the obstacles, meet the challenges, and climb onward toward the peak are rewarded with the panoramic view. What we long for is that—comprehensive awareness of all life as one, the experience of completion and fulfillment, a unity of our seeing, knowing, and living. In this clarity of understanding lies our true freedom.

According to Gurudev Shree Chitrabhanu, the great masters were those who, like a doctor, knew just where to operate to remove the cataract, the confusion in thinking. Because they stood at the peak, the height of self-mastery, they were able to show others the way. In this book, Gurudev draws upon his own thirty-eight years of experience in meditation to bring to life ancient reflections on twelve different facets of reality known as *bhava-*

nas. The insights which have arisen from his authenticity of experience and which he shares with us here can help us stop clinging to a distorted or dogmatic view and correct our vision.

To the Jains, the ultimate experience of reality is one, universal, unfragmented. Like a perfect diamond, it is radiant, luminous, reflecting its source, that in each of us which is flawless, enlightened, pure, conscious.

When that conscious reality comes into manifestation, it has a multitude of facets, countless rays of wisdom. Individually, each living being experiences that heart of the Self in his or her own unique way. That is why an integral part of the Jain philosophy and practice is *anekantavada,* a deep respect for others' viewpoints, an honest appreciation of the complementary nature of many approaches to truth. Behind this recognition, there is the feeling of wordless oneness which experiences the unity amidst all diversity. As the third in a trilogy of Gurudev's books, *Twelve Facets of Reality: The Jain Path to Freedom* reflects this principle, for it complements and completes its companion volumes, *Realize What You Are: The Dynamics of Jain Meditation,* and *The Psychology of Enlightenment: Meditations on the Seven Energy Centers.* Supportive to one another, these books take a person from the beginning steps in meditation to progressively deeper levels of practice and greater dimensions of awareness of life.

Gurudev's purpose in elucidating the *bhavanas* is to offer contemplations, pathways, open windows from which to see and feel the freshness of life. In each chapter, Gurudev presents a different pair of angles of vision, different facets of reality. When you plunge into the meaning of each one, a moment comes and your mind calms down. It hushes its chatter and ceases to breed dissension, friction, doubt and fear. It stops clinging to the past and fantasizing about the future. It disengages.

When the mind is not engaged, it is possible for you to have a genuine experience of reality. There is silence, space, receptivity. The glimpse strikes home and you bask in uncluttered awareness, in wonder and ecstasy. At that point, the window drops its frames and you are one with infinite vision. This is how these twelve facets can help you, as they have helped Jain monks for thousands of years, to take a leap beyond all limitations into your own vivid pulsating life.

Once Gurudev's master told him, "I can give you the maps, the teachings, the guidelines, the steps, but I cannot give you the eyes." Underlying these twelve contemplations is the same statement. Are you eager to grow? Are you willing to give up pain and suffering? Do you long to open your eyes and see clearly? If you have this quest for freedom, take this map in heart and mind. With patience and energy, enthusiasm and confidence, you can reach the peak.

In Gurudev's words, "For those who open themselves, there is transformation, from age to youth, from misery to joy, from pain to peace, from dwelling on one's mortal frame to feeling one's immortal life."

It has been a privilege and a joy to work on these chapters which were originally a series of twelve talks given by Gurudev to his students at the Jain Meditation International Center from March 2 to May 18, 1977. I am deeply grateful to three special people who gave to this book their loving help, enthusiasm, and spirit: John Miller and Richard Kleifgen, who went over the text with a careful and caring eye, and June Fogg, who coordinated many of the details which enabled this project to come to completion. In particular, a warm word of appreciation to Allan, my husband, for continuing to understand, accept, and give me the loving space I never had to ask for in order to concentrate on and complete this endeavor.

To Gurudev Shree Chitrabhanuji who has shared with us all this gift of his experience, insights, and ancient teachings, and to you, fellow travelers on the path to freedom, I bow, in deep reverence, friendship, and love.

—Clare Rosenfield

Twelve Facets of Reality

FACET ONE

The Changeless Beneath the Changes

IN this course we are going to meditate and reflect on twelve different facets of reality. Reflecting on these aspects, we will come closer to seeing life as it really is. When our mind does not see life as it is, it acts and reacts according to its preconceived concepts of what should be. It then uses all its energy to make these concepts concrete.

When concepts become concrete, then life becomes rigid, like a crystal. Whenever life becomes crystallized, there is no flow. Because of rigidity, we take stands. We go to the extent of fighting in order to maintain our bias. As a result, we become either temporarily happy or temporarily unhappy. If we watch ourselves at such times, we can see that we have lost pliability. In this way, we lose touch with the flow of life.

The twelve facets upon which we will meditate are twelve steps leading to the experience of reality. They are meant to awaken our inner awareness. In ancient days, they were called *bhavanas,* or reflections. Originally, they were given as meditation subjects to the Jain monks, to the initiates who had just left the worldly life with which they were familiar and whose taste was still upon their lips. They were to steep themselves in these meditations in order to remove this taste from their consciousness and come out from inertia, anxiety, distraction, moods, and desires. Absorbing and ruminating the meaning, they would come to penetrate the depths of their own reality.

Now these same *bhavanas* are offered to you, the serious students, the genuine seekers, to help you overcome the coverings and delusions which prevent you from seeing life as it is. The first and greatest stumbling block to confront and examine is *trushna,* or craving. Craving arises in your unawareness when you do not see an object as a thought crystal but, rather, as a means to gratify your desire. Then you put all your energy into getting it. Sometimes you never get it, and sometimes you do. But in any case, the time comes when you have to leave it. If you are aware when you have it in your palm, you look at it and smile at yourself, saying, "Is this the thing I have used so much effort to get? For this I have spent my energy?"

What attracts and allures you from a distance does not look the same at close range. When you go nearer, you wonder, "Is this the same as what I saw from a distance?" You might have noticed at some time that when you are far from a mountain, it appears mellow, round, and soft. Covered in mist, it looks like wax. When you are right next to it, though, you see the sharp stones and rocks.

That is why, in order to understand the nature of reality, we have to see what is real without distorting or hiding it. We have to remove all the outside wrappings which are created by our mind. The mind creates many beautiful phrases and mirages. It likes to hide reality with glossy coverings. Like the deer who runs toward a mirage of water when it is thirsty, we too are in a frenzy to get that which is merely an illusion.

If you want to feel the refreshing touch of a lake in summer, you have to remove your clothes. Otherwise, you will not get direct contact with the cool water. In the same way, if you want to enjoy the freshness of life, you must shed your coverings. Words, concepts, beliefs, crystallized thoughts act as coverings. Puncture them and you will see how hollow and insubstantial they are. Remove them and you will see yourself.

So the initiates are taught that they are deluded by outside things. They are given symbolic things to watch. For example, at dusk, the master and student may go out and sit and meditate. When it is monsoon season, there are clouds in many colors. Sometimes there is a rainbow. The master might tell the student, "See the beauty. Experience these colors. Notice in each cloud a shape. Be in tune with nature. Forget everything else. Then close your eyes."

The student becomes attuned to the colors and the shapes of the clouds at dusk. Then he closes his eyes and brings the picture of this to his mental eye. Over and over, he opens his eyes, watches the changing scene of nature, closes his eyes, and meditates.

After two hours, everything becomes dark. Then the teacher asks, "What do you see?"

The student answers, "I see nothing. Everything has gone."

Then the teacher asks, "Where have they gone—the beauty, the shapes, the clouds, the colors?"

The student remains in silence, pondering. And yet there is an answer. The beauty, the rainbow, have gone and yet they have not gone. They are there in a way. This is the point of meditation: everything is still there in the universe.

The teacher tells the student, "Nothing h
erything is there. But because of the rot

earth, you see changes. Your physical eye sees that something has gone.

"Now use your inner perception. See that the whole galaxy is moving in an unbroken rhythm. The same sun we think of as vanishing here is being seen across the globe as rising. And yet it is the same sun. Lift yourself above the level of earth to the height of the sun. You will always see the sun. Be conscious of that sun in you, there is changeless life in you."

Behind the continuous changes is the continuity of the changeless. Changes themselves indicate the ever-presence of the changeless.

As soon as a dry leaf drops, a new green leaf is already sprouting. If we are aware, we realize that behind the tiny new leaf there is changeless, vibrant life. Because of that life, one form is dropped and another emerges. And the soul of the old leaf has already gone on to a new form, one with more sensory equipment with which to perceive the world in a new, more sensitive way.

We begin to see that all life longs to move to higher realms of awareness. For that, change is inevitable. Change is what allows the changeless to reveal itself as ever fresh. Without it, there is no growth, no renewal.

When we become convinced that change is for growth and growth is for becoming aware of our inner divinity, we will be inspired to be free, free from the tendency to cling to familiar things. We will become eager to unshackle ourselves from the fear of change.

When this truth sinks into our consciousness, it opens a new door. We stop seeing in a rigid way. The words "gone," "disappear," "vanish," "death" are seen for what they are—as empty or misleading words, based purely on our visual perception, not on our inner insight. So what appears as "death" to one is "birth" to another; both are two waves of the same ocean: life.

So the teacher explains to the student, "Changes are causing us to be aware of the changeless, and the changeless is causing all the changes to take place. Until we reach the 'best,' we pass through 'good' and 'better.' All the forms change in order to bring out a better and better form. Ultimately, we become so refined as to be able to experience the radiance of our inner reality, the permanent bliss of our being. So, as you grow, cultivate this awareness—that in the sunset dawn is hidden, in the dawn sunset is hidden. Appearing and disappearing are the play of life. Both are manifestations of the changeless."

The reflection on this first point of meditation is called *anitya*—meaning transient, ever-changing—and *nitya*—meaning permanent, changeless. For the mind to know the ever-moving nature of *anitya* is frightening. Why? Because the mind tends to take that which is temporary and believe that it is going to last forever. The mind clings to whatever it has created—things, objects, ideas, relationships, positions. That is why it is not ready to give them up when the time comes. Such a mind says, "It is going to remain with me. It is mine now." But the nature of nature replies, "Nothing is thine and nothing is mine."

If it becomes yours, it is going to lose its nature. It will lose its capacity to change. If it loses its nature of change, it will lose its freshness of life. It will become stagnant. If it always remains summertime, you long for winter. If heat remains permanently high, you cannot bear it. In the same way, when winter becomes too prolonged, you dream of summer. Changes make everything new and fresh.

We have to re-educate our mind. Otherwise it tends

toward attachment, thereby creating sadness. When things or people depart from us, our mind is not ready to accept it. Grasping, the mind kills the spirit of the relationship. People accept this truth more readily for others than for themselves.

Observe what happens when the mind is not attached. Once an employee in a factory received a telegram telling him that his mother had died. He wanted to take a week's leave to go to his hometown to console his relatives and to be consoled by them. When he went to the factory owner to ask permission for the leave, the owner was out to lunch. So the employee left his telegram on the owner's desk, went back to his work, and waited.

It happened that the factory owner's mother was ill, and when he returned to his desk, without reading the name on the telegram, he saw only the words, "Your mother expired." Immediately he became sad and depressed. He put his head down on his desk and began crying.

When the employee came back, he saw right away that his telegram had caused a misunderstanding. He wanted to clear it up, so he explained, "Sir, please, I came to ask for leave because my mother expired." The owner looked up and said, "Your mother has also expired?" "No, sir," the employee explained, "I put that telegram on your desk when you were not here. It is my mother who has expired, not yours."

"It is your mother, not mine?" The owner jumped up, and in a matter of seconds he had become light and happy again. His whole attitude changed.

"Yes, sir," the employee continued. "Please grant me leave to see my relatives."

Now all of a sudden the owner began to preach and moralize because it was not his mother. He said, "Why do you want to waste your time going there? She is gone, and everything in the world leaves us sooner or later. Why make yourself so unhappy?"

See how the mind can teach beautiful truths to others when it is not bound by attachment. When you weave a thread around something, you are caught by it. This is the way the mind acts. Even the smallest thing which breaks, changes, or goes away can make you lose your balanced mood. Why? Because on that thing you have placed a seal and labeled it "mine."

Now, if you don't weave a thread around things that are not related to you, and if you know how to be wise for others, why do you not train your own mind not to cling and be possessive? Why do you not take a loss in your life as lightly as you would have others take it when it happens to them? Why are there two laws—one for you and one for others?

When you have a toothache, you feel as if there were an earthquake in your head. But when a real earthquake occurs, you merely comment, "This is the law of nature." Why do you feel no effect? Because of your emphasis on "I" and "my," you have lost connection with life at large. You have put all your energy into your own need, greed, and attachment. You have placed importance only on preserving the cocoon you have built around yourself.

Because of the cocoon, you become sad, depressed, angry. The slightest word, gesture, or insult can upset your whole day. Yet in your callousness, you can insult others and not remember. Why? Because there is no connection with the universal. All is centered selfishly in the mind, and that mind is not permanent. It is ever-changing.

So the master tells the monk, "Meditate on *nitya* and *anitya.* Find out what is permanent and what is impermanent. Separate the grain from the chaff. Now they are mixed together. You must winnow. Learn how to fan out the husk from the genuine kernel. Then you are able to know what is everlasting and what is temporary."

This process of winnowing is an inside process. For that you have to come to the center of yourself. First realize and accept the transitory nature of forms. Then you will experience the nature of nature, the changeless behind the ever-changing.

This winnowing makes you selective in your word, in your expression, in your relations. The phoniness goes away. You will not exclaim, "I will die for you!" It is easy to use such words, and yet nobody dies for anyone. It is only make-believe. People die for their own attachment, not for another person.

Before you use a word, feel the word. Taste the word. Just as a person who hears the word "mango" gets a taste and desire for mango in his mind, you get the real feeling of the word in your being. When you really experience the truth of this, then every word comes directly from your experience. You are not in a hurry to be clever with words.

There have been great poets and writers who did not write a lot, but when they did write they experienced deep feeling. They felt what they were bringing out. Whatever they wrote emerged from the depths. And what comes from the depths becomes immortal. Such words carry the touch of immortality.

Now we move deeper into self-investigation. By winnowing the chaff from the grain, by revealing the authenticity of our feeling with each word, we come to what we call "I." Who is this "I"? Is it a temporary "I" which is there for some eighty to ninety years? When the body ceases to function, where does it go? Has it gone into darkness or does it have some deeper significance of immortality?

Most people don't know what this "I" is even though they put it in capital letters. When we say, "I want to see you and talk to you," who do we mean? Do we mean "I" the body, the senses? Are we saying, "My senses want to see you"?

Is there only the body? Or is there something beyond? After all, when the doctor declares that a person is dead, the body is still there, the sense organs are still there. But the conscious, sentient energy that was able to sense is no longer dwelling in that body. Everything you might have thought of as "I" is still there. So what has gone? One minute ago, there was hope. Now the doctor says, "There is no hope." What has changed? Is there another "I" other than the "I" of body and senses which has gone from the body?

Go directly to yourself and ask, "What is that which has gone? What do I mean by 'I love you'—is it the body?"

If so, then why do we put it into a casket? Why do we not keep it? With chemicals we can preserve the body, but we don't want to keep it. Why do we not have the same feeling of communication and aesthetic outlook, the same feeling of love and ecstasy toward a body that is missing the real "I"?

What is missing and where has it gone? That "something" has not ceased to exist. If it has, then the world becomes nothing but constant change, impermanence.

But there is the changeless; essence remains. Only in a particular moment, for a particular person, does it seem no longer to exist. It only appears as though dusk with its beauty and glow has disappeared. And yet we know it has not gone permanently. Dusk is somewhere, in some new form.

If you take a plane which travels at two thousand miles per hour, you can catch the glow of the sun. You can keep up with it and see that it has not gone anywhere. Catching up to it, you will be able to go farther than dusk, farther even than the sun.

We say that the sun rises and sets, but we know that the sun does neither. The movement of the earth is what gives us the illusion of the sun's rising and setting. The words we use are not precise. In the same way, in reality, we cannot say that the "I" disappears. As soon as it seems to be gone, it has already taken another shape, another glow, another color. When someone is crying over the loss of somebody, already that somebody is making someone else happy! In some house, happiness is bubbling, and someone is realizing, "Oh, I am pregnant!"

What has gone? What has come? Only the forms, the garbs, the houses. Not this "I." This "I" is moving eternally from beginningless time, becoming more and more aware of its reality through the evolution of form. The whole universe is a means to reach ultimate freedom.

When someone goes from your sight, remember the relation, the communication you had. To accept with solemnity and understanding is different from resisting with depression and sadness. To accept with calmness and deep feeling is not the same as crying, falling into deep mourning, and losing interest in life. People cry and sink to the bottom because of dependency. There was a crutch to lean on, and now that crutch has gone. People mourn not the person but the crutch. Where can they lean now?

It is not so easy to change thinking patterns. We live

in a world of concepts, beliefs, and taboos. These are the walls and coverings preventing us from seeing and experiencing the real "I" of ourselves and others.

There is a beautiful example of a young monk named Upagupta. It was nighttime during the rainy season, and the path in the forest was covered with a blanket of darkness. Upagupta found his way to a certain tree and sat down to meditate.

It happened at that time that a famous dancer was going through the same forest to meet her beloved. The darkness was so thick that she could not see where she was going. She was still trying to feel the track underfoot when she bumped into Upagupta.

"Oh!" she exclaimed. "Who is this human being?"

Just then there was a flash of lightning. In that flash she saw the person she had accidentally come up against.

"Such a beautiful person is sitting there," she thought. "So calm and serene he is. His lovely face and body look as though they were carved out of pure marble. Oh, if I get this man, this will be heaven on earth!"

She was proud of her beauty. She was the most famous dancer of her time and men would flock to her feet. She said, "You are so calm. You have such a radiance. Please come with me."

When he did not respond, she shook him and said, "You are meditating on what? See who I am!" Upagupta recognized the dancer. "I know who you are. But this is not the time, though I know that you love me. You go on your way. I will see you one day."

The dancer thought, "He knows I love him, he says. Then why delay?"

So she spoke to him again. "What is the reason for postponing? It will be too late. This is the right time."

He answered, "I know it, but the right time has not

come in the right way. I promise you I will meet you. And remember, as you love, I too love. When it is the right time, I will come."

The dancer thought he was not in his right mind. And she went on.

Youth is like lightning, like a shadow, like the flow of water, ever-moving, so swift. Ten years passed. The dancer had overused her energy of youth and was now exhausted. She had not taken care of her body and was now suffering from a skin disease. She was trembling with fever and there were blisters on her skin. Nobody would even look at her, and the king drove her from the town. She was compelled to go out to a deserted village and live in a tiny hovel. There she was wasting away, crying and alone.

The time was right and a man came to see her there. He took her head in his lap. She was shivering with fever as he applied medicine to her sores, mouth, and head.

"Who are you?" she mumbled.

"I am Upagupta. Do you remember? I promised you. I love you. I have come to take care of you."

"Now I don't have anything to offer you," she moaned.

"No," he told her, "at that time you had something to offer which was transient, something which you yourself could not keep. Now you have something real to offer. I love that which is not going to go. Our relation is for that. It is the relation of soul.

"In the glamour and ego of the past years, you did not realize the changing nature of all that—of your body, beauty, wealth, and your circle of partying friends. They were all there because there was that need. They were feeding it and now that need is over. My need is not that. Mine is the need of the soul."

Tears started rolling down the dancer's cheeks. She

began sobbing. All ignorance was washed away by her tears. Upagupta took great care of her.

"Now," he told her, "let us transcend the small "I" and help others become aware of the real "I."

Soon the dancer recovered, and when she became healthy and strong, she renounced her old life and became a student of Upagupta. She spent the rest of her days peacefully meditating and sharing her insights with others.

When we are not aware of the real "I" in us, we are continually engaged in trying to keep the unreal "I" intact. The artificial "I" is the one created by society, emotions, and needs. It is what we call the body "I," the name "I," the form "I." Whenever we sense some danger to this superficial "I," we become upset, angry, and depressed. We have a sense of fear. We are ready to do anything to protect this "I" which cannot be protected.

The intrinsic nature of the superficial "I" is to change. That is why there is fear. Something in us knows that this "I" does not have the quality of permanence. If we identify totally with the ever-changing "I," we don't have that fearlessness which comes from knowing that in us which is changeless.

What we need is that fearlessness. It can only unfold in us when we know the real "I" and its permanence, when we know the difference between *nitya* and *anitya.* By knowing the "I" which is real, we are sure it is going to remain. Once we know it is not going to go anywhere, we don't make any effort to keep it.

It is like the difference between a candle and an electric lamp when you stand by the window. Near the window the candle is always flickering in the wind, so you put a protective covering over it. That is like the unreal "I" which we are constantly trying to protect, though it cannot be preserved permanently. But if you have an electric lamp, you have no need to protect it. You are not afraid that it will go out. The wind cannot extinguish it. The real "I" is like this, secure in all circumstances.

From where does this superficial "I" come? It is created, built by karmas, customs, creed. It is a social "I." Because of different geographical, physiological, and emotional programming, it creates barriers among people. Your unreal "I" is not the same as someone else's because what is important for your nation, race, or society is not important for his. So our mental structures and emotional needs are relative. And what is relative cannot become permanent.

That is why wise people don't try to impose their values on others. They see things as they are. They know the difference between the social "I" and the real "I." They are aware that the temporary "I" is a product of their conditioning and their society's values. Going further, they see something transcending. The transcending "I" has no local or geographical limitations. It has no fear of losing. That "I" is *nitya,* ever-remaining, immortal. That "I" is in you. That "I" is in me. That "I" is in everyone.

Your relationships must begin with yourself. First you know that "I" in you, then you will see it in everybody. If you cannot see the real "I" in you, you won't be able to see it in anybody.

Taking time to know it does not mean you are selfish. It means that you are experimenting with truth on yourself first. Then you will be able to share it with others. Before you give something hot to someone, don't you first test it on your own skin? In the same way, before you give this truth to someone, first experience it yourself.

So in the light of this meditation, see your own reality. Throw off the outside coverings and see the inside substance. Observe that until now you have made a box around yourself. Now you want to know what is really inside. If you don't go to your reality, your whole life will be nothing but pretense and fantasy. Living in make-believe, you will not be able to take the last step of evolution. So if you want to go further, be genuine. Go beyond words and come to the truth of experience.

See that although "I" appears to change with the change, in reality it is changeless. When people depart from you or you depart from them, see with the knowledge that something in you both will stay, something in you will meet again. As understanding deepens, relationships become profound. They are not only of the body, but they are perfumed with essence.

Otherwise, life is filled with so much fear and anxiety that it is unbearable. But if you know that essence is never lost, though you feel sadness at a dear one's departure, still you can come back to your work, continue your routine, and experience living fully. Though there is seeming disappearance, this disappearance is in order to appear somewhere else. In order to go there, you have to leave here. In pure relationship one companion goes ahead of the other. The other follows later. The parting is temporary. They meet again. The changeless indicates that which cannot die, for it was never born; it is the very life of life.

Meditating in this way, we develop a sense of discrimination and a vast vision. Small things which used to trigger our addictions no longer bother us. There will be no need to use so much energy on temporary things. We become generous toward the shortcomings of others. We start to experience a deep feeling of oneness with all life, and we will not cry over the spilt milk of transitoriness. With our inner vision, we see that which is continuously pulsating in all, and rejoice.

◈ Seed-Thoughts for Meditation

If I accept rather than deny the transitory nature of all forms, then I can go deeper and realize that there is changeless life behind the ever-changing.

Change is for growth, and growth is for change. Both are for helping us become aware of our inner divinity and for inspiring us to move into higher life.

Let me stop trying to preserve the temporary cocoon I have built around myself so that I can connect to life at large.

Something in us will stay. That I love. It is the relation of soul to soul.

Appearing and disappearing are the play of life. Both are two waves of the same ocean. Both are there to reveal reality in a new and fresh way.

FACET TWO

Our Protection in an Unprotected World

JUST as we need food for our body to nourish it, so we need food for the nourishment of our mind. When our mind does not get good thoughts, positive ideas, which are its nutrition, it becomes weak. And just as a weak body becomes the victim of any disease or virus, in the same way a weak mind can become the victim of any influence. It becomes impressionable, and wherever it goes, it takes on the color of that influence. It doesn't have its own special way of thinking.

A weak mind is more dangerous than a weak body. If somebody has a weak body, it is noticeable, and he can take vitamins, proper food, or yoga postures to strengthen it. But if the mind becomes weak, it is not so easily noticed.

Ultimately, the strength of the mind helps strengthen the body; and together they help the soul on its journey. That is why these twelve reflections are given—to use mind and body for the journey of soul, to use meditation to uncover that which is permanent, to see life as it is.

Meditation can be used also for only temporary things—to feel good, to get wealth, to have pleasant relationships. If you offer these reflections to those who want only the temporary, they will reject them. Why? Because they are not ready to go deep. They want what they can get immediately.

We are talking of something permanent, of long-term things in which some people have no interest. Those whose quest for the permanent has not yet awakened think, "Who knows what will happen later, after fifty years? Let me enjoy now!"

So the twelve reflections are given to the initiates, to people who are sincerely interested in life and the life to come; or, let us say, in the flow of life. Those who have given us these *bhavanas* saw the continuity of life, the eternal flow. They didn't start with birth or end with death. For them birth is a wave and death is another wave. If you ask, "Where is the first wave?" the wise ones answer, "It exists in the second wave. Show me the first wave and see the second wave. The first wave has created the second wave."

If you want to know the existence of the first wave, then you have to know the second wave. If the first wave has not subsided, then the second wave will not come. *The coming of another wave itself indicates that the previous wave has already merged. Something merges and something emerges.* This is the whole process—merge and emerge. So birth is nothing but somewhere else a death. One wave merges in death, and another wave emerges in birth.

These two waves are connected deeply with one another. When we start experiencing this deep truth, this deep instinct, not only in words or phrases but in our real experience, we are then able to live in this world in the state of fearlessness. We can use all the techniques to overcome fear, but as long as we remain on a level of quotations without experience, the fear remains. Why do people have fear? Because they see everything decaying, disappearing. They have not gone beyond this level. That is why fear is always at the back of their mind.

This meditation helps us gradually experience another approach, a space where fear does not exist. How is this possible? Because the consciousness starts experiencing the permanent behind all the impermanence. It starts seeing the merging of the wave in the emergence of another wave.

Someone may say, "The thing has disappeared." The person who has meditated will answer, "You talk of disappearing. Do you not see something appearing? Why emphasize that which is lost? Why do you not see that which is gained?" That is why our first meditation was on the changeless behind the changes. The world you see is ever-moving. It moves and that is why it is new and fresh. But our ignorant mind wants to hold on to the things as they were and keep them. The mind has the habit of turning everything into an antique; it loves antiques!

When you have realized the difference between the permanent and the transient exactly, then you are ready to come to the second reflection—*asharana,* meaning unprotectedness. Beyond that is *sharana,* meaning protection. The initiate thinks, "I am always trying to seek some protection, some savior. My mind has been comfortable when somebody was leading me, taking care of me. Now I know that what I cannot do for myself nobody will do for me." This reflection gives a new insight—not to be dependent.

Mental dependence is built from childhood. If the mother goes away, the baby cries. It is natural. But even in their sixties people are like babies crying when mother leaves. Why? Because they always have that feeling of helplessness. They aren't ready to stand on their own feet.

When you see that on which you were leaning slipping away, watch the fear arise. See how panic overtakes you. This second meditation helps us see that other people, and things as well, are themselves helpless. How can they help you when they too are helpless?

In reality, as long as you have the appropriate karmas, the person or thing will remain with you. You may do a hundred things to hold on, but when the karmas are over, the thing will go. And if you are not ready to see the truth, you may crumble completely. You find that it was a prop, a support, or a crutch. When you completely lean upon a prop or a crutch, what happens when it breaks? You tumble down. The idea is to build your inner muscles. Meditation, if rightly digested, gives you great strength. You start building inner power.

This does not mean you never accept anybody's help. It means you don't depend on it. If any help comes, take it, appreciate it, and be thankful for it. The difference is this: if you are not dependent, and help does not come, you do not mind; but if you are dependent, and help does not come, you wait and build expectation. When your expectation is not fulfilled, you feel fear and panic. "What will happen now? Who is mine?"

There is a meaningful story in Jain tradition about a young monk who had come to understand *asharana* in his life. One beautiful morning, he was sitting under a tree meditating. In that era the king of that area was Bimbisara, who was also in his youth, and very handsome. At the time, he was full of ego, for he did not know anything about religion, spirituality, or the inside world. He gloried in his own youthful strength and prosperity. He was the biggest king of Magadha, now known as Bihar. On this morning, as Bimbisara was riding along on his horse, the birds were chirping, the flowers were blossoming, and nature was in full bloom.

Riding by, he saw the monk sitting under the tree meditating, and thought, "Why is this young man sitting and meditating here? He must be engulfed in poverty. Let me help him." So he called out, "Young man, what are you doing here? You appear like a mendicant."

"Yes, sir," answered the young monk.

"What is your name?" the king inquired.

"My name is Anatha, the unprotected one. I am protectionless."

The king was shocked. "When a king like me is lord of this whole province, how can you call yourself Anatha, kingless?"

"Sir," answered the monk, "shall I tell you my story? Do you have patience?"

"Yes," said the king eagerly. "I would like to hear you."

This is the story he related. "I was in my twenties and I had a beautiful wife, a big family, wealth, a beautiful house, plenty of money, food, and jewelry. All loved me, and at that time I was in the full bloom of youth. I became so egotistical and proud of myself I would not look down. I thought that the world must be at my feet. 'Whatsoever I desire, the world brings to me,' is the way I used to think.

"This ego I continued building inside. As a result, I continued treating other people as nothing.

"Then one day I came home from a walk in the garden and felt a little uncomfortable. I got a headache and fever. Slowly the fever increased. By night I was in bed. My body was shivering. My mother, who loved me, said, 'My darling son, what can I do for you? I am helpless. Let me bring something.'

"Physicians came, the herbalist came—but nothing helped.

"Here were so many people caring for me, but they could not protect me. Each pore was burning like fire. I was crying. Sir, Bimbisara, hear me! I was so helpless! And my wife, who loved me from her heart, prepared and applied sandalwood paste to cool my body. But as soon as it dried up, again the burning started. So it was applied for two, three, and four hours at a time. And then even that was too much, and it led to too much cold.

"Sir, will you believe it? In twenty-one days I became a skeleton and I could not digest any food or medicine. At that time, I thought, 'What shall I do?' I became desperate, and although my wife, mother, and servants were there, I was alone in the bed, without any refuge or strength to turn to.

"Then a thought came to my mind. Once when I was going somewhere on my horse, the great sage Mahavir was speaking and I heard him as I was passing by. He said, 'When you are helpless and there is no protection, accept the protection of these four pure elements: *Arihanta*—those who have conquered all inner weaknesses; *Siddha*—the Perfect Souls; *Sahu*—the Saints, whose energy is vibrating in the universe; *Dharma*—the Pure Teaching which comes from the Enlightened Ones. With pure feeling, move toward that. When there is no protection, take the protection of these four.'

"This idea came floating to my mind. I thought, 'Now that nobody is able to protect me, let me surrender myself to this.' My mind became so engaged in repeating these blessed words that I started absorbing the energy.

"Exactly at midnight, my eyes were so calm and clear that I was able to sleep peacefully the whole night. In the morning when my wife saw me, she thought, 'Last night

I applied sandalwood paste especially and now I see it has worked.' And the doctor thought, 'My medicine is working now.' Another came and said, 'I gave roots and now the juice from them is working on him.' Everyone was ready to take credit for my improvement.

"In the afternoon, when I opened my eyes, everyone started to tell me what they were thinking. I told them, 'Thank you for what you have done for me. I appreciate your care and your help and your feelings. But let me tell you the truth: in this world when a person becomes protectionless, there is nevertheless one protection: the Higher Self.'

"I connected to that invisible inner force, which is always there, and ultimately I became in tune with it. My mind which was creating so many turbulent thoughts became calm. In the state of calmness, I merged into that pure state, and I thought, 'I take protection of all the Perfect Souls who became pure consciousness. I associate with their vibrations. I take refuge in the Conquerors of inner weaknesses. I join myself with the Saints of the universe wherever they are. And I merge in that Teaching of *Dharma,* that flow which comes from the compassion, love, and deep peace of the Omniscient Ones.

"That turned into medicine. It became a soothing balm for my consciousness."

Then Bimbisara asked, "What did you do then?"

"After that," the monk continued, "when I became well, I decided to take another path. I left my prosperous life. I have taken the path of the unprotected. That is why I am Anatha, without any worldly resort or master. But if you want to know the spiritual master, it is Arihanta Mahavir."

"Who is Mahavir?" asked the king.

"Sir, fifteen miles from here, in your town of Rajagruha, he is living a beautiful life. Go there and see for yourself."

Because of the young man's word, Bimbisara went to visit Mahavir and then and there became his disciple. He became his patron as well, and throughout his life he supported both Mahavir and Buddha, who also came to live and teach in the region at that time. Bimbisara devoted his life to supporting the teachings and all the good causes because he felt it was his mission.

When we meditate on unprotectedness, we gain a different level of understanding. We see that the real help comes from the pure stream of consciousness. It is like a current that is always flowing. When we need it, we will have it. It is always there. We have only to remove the curtain and open ourselves to that energy whose nature is infinite knowledge, infinite bliss, and infinite vision. We have only to turn our consciousness inward to connect with life. It is our *sharana,* our wellspring, our reserve strength, our invisible refuge, which will not exhaust itself at any time.

If you are able to connect with this source, then you are not helpless, for you are protected from within. As soon as you start knowing this protection, you start lifting yourself. The sinking boat begins to float.

Use this meditation as the young monk Anatha and King Bimbisara did. Take time to go on watching and pondering. Whenever fear comes, ask, "Why am I afraid? What is this anxiety? What is the cause of the fear? The cause is that I am not connected to my invisible world."

Build inner strength and power by connecting to the invisible world of these vibrations. Chant aloud or silently the entire *mantra* as follows.

Cattari Mangalum	These are the Four Blessings.
Arihanta Mangalum	Conquerers of inner weaknesses are blessing.
Siddha Mangalum	Perfect Souls are blessing.
Sahu Mangalum	Saints are blessing.
Kevali Pannato Dhammo Mangalum	The Teaching which has come from the Omniscient Ones is blessing.
Cattari Loguttama	These Four are supreme, unsurpassed.
Arihanta Loguttama	*Arihanta* are supreme.
Siddha Loguttama	*Siddha* are supreme.
Sahu Loguttama	Saints are supreme.
Kevali Pannato Dhammo Loguttamo	The Teaching which has come from the Omniscient Ones is supreme.
Cattari Sharanum Pavajjami	These are the Four Protections.
Arihante Sharanum Pavajjami	I go to the protection of the *Arihanta.*
Siddhe Sharanum Pavajjami	I go to the protection of the *Siddha.*
Sahu Sharanum Pavajjami	I go to the protection of the *Sahu.*
Kevali Pannatum Dhammum Sharanum Pavajjami	I merge with the Pure Teaching—Non-Violence, Peace, Love, Compassion.

When your small self merges with these four protections, the Higher Self, your reality, emerges.

SEED-THOUGHTS FOR MEDITATION

I am becoming aware of unprotectedness. One by one, I see that the things and persons on whom I depend are themselves helpless.

Let me turn my consciousness away from the temporary dependencies and connect with the pure stream of life which is prevailing. Merging with that consciousness, I find my everlasting protection, my inner world.

Let me experience the eternity of life, the eternal flow. That one wave has come means another wave has subsided. Birth is nothing but somewhere else a death. So this is the process—something merges so that something else may emerge.

⸎ FACET THREE

Liberation from the Cycle of Birth and Death

TO make room in our heart for truth, we have to clear away the clutter of false thinking. For that we need guidance, reflections. With introspection, we are able to see what is real, genuine, lasting. Using our inner eye, we are able to come out from under the domination of distorted thinking.

Why do we live in a world of make-believe? Why do we create so many fantasies? To protect ourselves from fear. Why are we afraid? Because something in us knows that the mind is weak and has the nature to disintegrate. The mind tends to scatter and jump from subject to subject, from form to form. Subconsciously, it has fear of its own decomposition.

In order not to be diffused or disintegrated, the mind seeks protection—in the husband and wife, lover and beloved, parent and savior. It relaxes under this false sense of security. It does not realize that this kind of outer protection is merely a prop. In search of some kind of shelter, we create a fence around ourselves. We may call this fence love, but in reality it is attachment. It is attachment covered up and decorated with beautiful outer wrappings of papery-thin love.

In each person's life the time comes when the mind scatters like a castle of cards. It stands firm so long as a gust of wind does not blow it down. When the reality of a crisis strikes, mind dips down. You feel depressed, rejected, and lonely. Life appears dismal and dark. You experience a state of hopelessness.

Wise people know that the shelter created by fantasy and outside props will not last. This kind of shelter is too fragile. What to do when you are again out in the open, naked, and without a roof over your head?

That is why we meditate on the *bhavanas.* They are a preparation. We build inner muscles with our awareness. Just as an athlete builds his muscles lifting weights, we build our inner strength with special tools. These tools are reflections, meaningful words, and insights.

You prepare yourself to know how to stand alone. And when you really know how to stand alone, you are all one. *You have only to go into the depth of aloneness to know the meaning of all-oneness.*

Not everyone is ready to do this. These facets are given only to those who are ready. Truth is dazzling. It has so much brilliance that weak eyes are not able to stand it. In the face of that brilliance, those with weak eyes do one of two things—either they turn away and change direction, or they cover their eyes with dark glasses.

But there are those who do want to see the truth. They say, "Let us see what may come." And ultimately what appears bitter turns out to be sweet honey. As you go on building inner strength, when the time comes for the support to go away, you won't tumble down.

Those who are eager to face truth reflect on the difference between attachment and love. In reflection, they see that attachment always comes with demands or conditions. Those who know how to stand back can notice it. Using their insight, they ask themselves, "Is what I am calling love really attachment thriving under the shelter of beautiful words? Do I have any demand on the person whom I love? Is it a kind of bargain? Is it a business?"

When we put love in the category of business, it is not love. In business, we see where we get profit. There is no feeling of giving, offering, accepting, only seeing who gets more. Both parties are watching out for themselves. If this is the case in a relationship, then are we not deluding ourselves?

So when you understand this truth, you understand your relationships. Your awareness becomes different. Your perception changes. You know how to give space, how to give room. Relationships become sweeter, more meaningful. Then the other party starts learning from you. Love is vast. When you encompass that vastness, then you love all. When you love all, then you *really* love the one whom you love.

It may not happen overnight. It is a slow movement, a gradual growth, not an instant answer or a temporary satisfaction. You need to have patience. My teacher told me: "First you have to learn how to stand on the ground of reality, of truth. That ground has no route. You have to make your own track. It's a vast territory before you. All directions are open. So don't tread the well-worn path. That only becomes a rut. Select your way over fresh open ground. Then you will be making a new track, fresh footprints."

Feel the newness. Tell yourself, "I am taking each step according to my insight." You can do it when you have faith in your feet and trust in your strength.

The third facet on which to reflect is called *samsara,* which means to move constantly up and down, down and up, in a smooth, circular, and rhythmical motion, like a Ferris wheel. It is a continuous process. When a person is motivated by greed for pleasure and power, he gets caught up in this perpetual motion and ends up where he began, like an ox circling around a treadmill. But the person with awareness of the purposeful direction of life can use each turn of the wheel for moving forward into evolution, for freeing himself from the need to rush after things which are on the periphery of life. So what is a cause of bondage to one can be used as a cause of freedom to another; it depends on the depth of one's understanding and approach. That is why this *bhavana* teaches the aspirant to watch the Ferris wheel of life, but not to identify with it.

We have all heard of prosperous famous families whose children lose everything and are forgotten. We have also observed those who, according to worldly standards, were "nobody" become "somebody." This wheel is always turning. It is an endless cycle. Sometimes we have days in which life is heavenly. Sometimes we have days in which life feels like a hell. The person you greet in the morning is not the same by evening. There are so many fluctuations in moods.

So the initiates watch the Ferris wheel. They see that the down will not remain down. It will go up. It will go on. Through watching, the initiate learns not to take the downs and ups seriously. "It is the wheel which is moving, not me," he observes. "I am sitting in the same seat. What is going up and down is the wheel, but I am here —steady."

Once you have this experience, you will see the game of life. The seriousness, the rejection, the clouds which cover your inner peace will be gone. And you will start enjoying life. Wherever you are and whomever you are with you experience and enjoy.

In this way, you slowly free yourself from identifying with the ups and downs of *samsara.* The wheel is always moving smoothly in order to bring change. With your awareness, you observe how it is moving purposefully to bring something beautiful, something fresh for you. The motion of the wheel is giving you a challenge. Without change, life becomes stagnant. If there is no test, there is no progress.

By identifying with the changeless beneath all the changes, you are transcending them. In this way, you experience the purpose of *samsara*—to transform yourself from lower to higher, and ultimately to reach *moksha,* complete freedom from the cycle of birth and death.

In meditating on this *bhavana,* we observe our whole cycle. We say, "When I was born, my mother was in pain, crying. Then she saw my face and was happy. The pain was gone." What the mother suffered for nine months was gone in one minute. At the same time, we look at those close to us in our lives—a brother, sister, parent, or partner—and see that some have gone and some are still here. The dearest people whom we love and who love us come and go. They don't remain permanently. The people who hate and are hated also come and go. This is the Ferris wheel; this is the process.

The reflection continues in this way: "Why do I only think of others? I also will go. I will move on, and when I do, I will separate from others as others have separated from me. So why am I upset when others depart? I too will depart. Perhaps I don't think of that because of the mental fright it causes."

But the aspirant is not frightened. His mind is not shattered at the prospect of his own departure. Why? Because he or she is completely convinced that what is permanent is not going to become impermanent. And what is impermanent is not going to become permanent. Each has its own nature. The seeker knows, "What I have at the center of myself is permanent. Only the house, the place, the dress, the form, will change. They are the persona, the mask, but the individual flame that I am does not change."

What confidence to know that! When it happens, for the first time you are realizing the difference between the husk and the grain. You see how deeply you have identified the grain with the husk. You observe how you have seen your own friends in this fixed, static light—as their persona instead of their essence.

If we relate only to the persona of an individual, the friendship is shallow. It is built on material gain. The person with a spiritual outlook sees things from a different vantage point. He sees that those things on which he once placed so much value are not truly valuable. They are tokens for use in a certain period, in a certain place. If you take a subway token to Russia, it cannot be used. It is meant to be used here. Similarly, the things of the world are to be used as tokens; they take you from one place to another. Beyond that they have no meaning.

Friendship based on the spiritual level remains permanent. Why? Because it has an inner connection, above and beyond its outside connection. In *The Last Days of Pompeii,* a volcano was about to erupt. An old man of greed and covetousness had jewels and gold coins hidden away in his house. There was scarcely enough time for him to run for his life; nevertheless, he went back to take his box of jewels. It was heavy, and his son, who was also greedy, said, "Father, let me carry the box for you. It is too heavy and you will not be able to run fast."

The old man did not trust his son even during that last moment. And the son became impatient and struck his father with a stick, grabbed the box, and ran. At that moment, the volcano erupted and the whole village was buried, father and son as well. Their relationship was superficial, based on need and greed. Their mutual protection was only to get material gain.

So become a spectator. See how the rich become poor, the young become old, the great become small. It is a joy to watch. The ornament changes but the gold remains.

Observe your form. It is beautiful. See who is in the center of your form, who animates all this. Who gives feeling to the body, allowing it to sense and to feel? Who gives voice to the throat and taste to the tongue? Who gives the sense of smell to the nose? Who gives light and sight to the eyes and hearing to the ears? Who gives awareness to the mind? When you realize that *you* are the one animating all your senses, you will stop accepting false beliefs and outside supports. You will have persuaded your doorkeeper mind to open the door and let you in—to see your own reality. Once you experience this changeless center of yourself, you exclaim, "That reality is here! That reality is I!"

Now you watch the circumference from the center. You observe life from that point which views all points. You are in a state of equanimity. You are not caught up with each turn of the wheel. In this way, you are free, not from past karmas which continue to move the wheel of *samsara* round and round, but from the ignorance which formerly made you cling to the changing elements themselves. Freed from the swings of mood, you glimpse the real freedom of *moksha.*

With this glimpse, you have the power to use your will to make decisions, to change what you want to change, even to heal your body. You know that you have at your disposal the energy which is your life force itself. It is the energy which animates this body, its senses and brain. Knowing it in your meditative experience, with patience and persistent practice you can mobilize this energy to erase your karmas and stop the cycle of birth and rebirth. With awareness, you can change wrong kinds of eating, thinking, and living. You can get rid of heavy negative vibrations which you have absorbed and which have turned into mental disturbance or physical disease. For one who realizes how such vibrations came and how they can be removed, the process of self-healing can be accelerated.

There is a story of a woman whose husband was constantly gambling and getting drunk. He used to come home late at night, knock on the door, and wait for his wife to open it. She would do so at whatever hour he came home. Always she remained peaceful, patient.

Eventually, he grew tired of his own vices and ran away. After five years, with spoiled health, he returned home. His wife had known that one day he would. Meanwhile, during the five years in which he had been absent, she had not lost her peace nor had she turned to vices herself. She had used her time to build her inner muscles.

She was so strong that the evening he returned and stood at the door, she only said, "Come in, please!" He could not believe that after five years, after having run away, he could be hearing these gentle words. Then she said, "You must be hungry. Have some dinner."

Hearing these sweetly spoken words, he began to melt inside. He started to cry. The tears kept on rolling down his cheeks. Gently his wife said, "Have I not told you—you are not bad. It was the company you kept. And don't these tears show that the core of your heart is good and soft?" He felt like bowing at her feet. "I have heard about saints," he said, "but if I had not seen you, I would never have believed. Now I know that I have no need to go away again." He then began moving forward into a purposeful life.

It is knowing your permanent reality which gives meaning to life. So meditate on your evolution and unite the world with your deep understanding of this. Let your real essence emerge and let outer superficiality melt away. This ground of truth has many routes; you create your own track. To reach your reality and feel your freedom, take a step which is full of positive feeling, radiant with light, and vibrant with awareness.

Seed-Thoughts for Meditation

The ever-moving is a continuous cycle of change, moving in a smooth and rhythmic motion. I am in the center, steady, aware.

Let me watch the circumference from the center. Let me observe the kaleidoscope of changes from that point which views all points.

Each turn of the wheel can be either a cause of my bondage or a cause of my freedom. With awareness, I can use each turn as a challenge, to free myself from karmas, to bring out transformation, to feel new life, and to lead me closer to my reality.

FACET FOUR

Freedom from Dependency

MOST people go through their lives not knowing what they want, yet sure that they did not get it. Because of that, they are sour and bitter. They go on grumbling even though they really do not know what they want. It appears a bit silly, but think of it. When you fall into a depressed frame of mind and someone asks you, "Why are you unhappy?" do you find the right cause of your unhappiness? Or do you start blaming something in general?

Let us probe this further. What is the real cause of unhappiness? Are outside things really deluding or tempting in themselves? Do they have the innate capacity to harass us or allure us? Or is it our addiction to them which makes us see them in that way?

It is our addiction which makes us blame outside things which, if we look closely, are themselves only things. We want to go beyond the blaming, beyond the addiction, beyond all these limiting conditions. That is our quest. We will not be satisfied with superficial answers or with a temporary boost. Genuine seekers do not spend their time in search of a mere "high." They know that like soda water when it is shaken, a temporary "high" will fall back down to the same state.

That is why we want to see both—the real and the

unreal, our essence and our addictions. The genuine teachers and teachings take us into the depth of reality and help us understand the nature of addiction. They encourage us to ask ourselves, "What is addiction? How have we built addictions around us? In what ways have we identified with them? Without them, does our life seem empty, miserable, and helpless?"

In order to see clearly, we meditate on the fourth facet, *ekatva. Ekatva* means One, and you have so many in your mind. Because of *bahutva,* or multiplicity, you don't see that One. Around that One everything is circling.

We can think of it in this way: We have a circumference and a center. The center is one, but on the circumference there are many. The circumference is so big and obvious that we don't have the insight to see the subtle center. That is why we are always moving on the circumference, outside of ourselves. That is why we look for some scapegoat to blame. We like to pin our unhappiness on somebody, saying, "If you were not in my life, my life would be heaven." Or we say it the other way around. "If you were in my life, my life would be heaven."

The circumference plays such an elusive role that one loses sight of the center. One must see that the whole circumference is made for the center, that if there were no center, a circumference could not exist.

See yourself for a while, looking from the center to the circumference. Until now your mind has been engaged twenty-four hours a day with *bahutva,* the circumference. Always somebody or something has been there engaging your mind—money, power, possessions, a friend, or a foe. That is why you are never completely with yourself. Even when you do sit down to be alone with yourself, even in that moment, something is there to distract you.

You act as though there were nothing in the center, as though everything were on the outside.

The tangible world does exist. It is the material half of our existence. In it we have trust. The problem arises when, instead of accepting this material world for what it is, we become obsessed by it. Then we neglect the invisible world. If something is not visible or tangible, then we don't have trust in it.

But we must open our minds and see that the visible depends upon the invisible. If there were no invisible, the visible would have no meaning. If there were no intangible, the tangible would have no feeling. The tangible cannot be felt without the intangible. The tangible is dear to us precisely because there is the intangible at the center of it.

Take, for example, a woman who wins first prize in a beauty contest. In all nations she becomes recognized as a universal beauty. Seeing her beauty, many people will want to marry her. They do not think of the soul inside this beautiful body. But one day her soul will leave its house. Her body will lie lifeless, and then even those who do not believe in soul will not be willing to marry her. Everything is still there—the eyes, ears, limbs, and shapes.

Why is it that now this tangible, visible body no longer has any attraction? Something surely has gone from it! The breath has gone. But who was operating the breath? Who was inhaling and exhaling? Who was in the center of that breath? Do you know? I tell you that that is what you have to come to know. When you meditate on this, you will discover the intangible which makes this tangible body living, pleasant, acceptable, and social.

When you see something in you beyond the physical aspect, your life will become very meaningful. You will begin to appreciate your human being–ness. You will change your attitude toward other people. You will not see only the physical body.

You will stop relating to people as objects. Your relationship will be that of the subject. Now you see someone only as an object and you do not feel oneness with the individual. When you see someone as the subject, you see the "I," the one who is.

When you experience "I am," you are living in your consciousness. There is no duality. As soon as you say "I want," desire begins. From desire comes the object. Now you are separating from the world. Out of the two, "I" and "want," a third thing comes, "the world"; "I want the world." This trinity is born from duality. The world out there is born every time you separate from the subject, your center, "I." As soon as you are out of your consciousness, duality is there, the world is there.

Ekatva means to realize ultimately "I am," not "I want." It means to break the concept of duality and be oneself. When you bring the whole world into "being," life merges into one flow. Then there is no manifestation of otherness, only oneness.

If you keep that essence in awareness, then seeing what you see does not create duality. You are not seeing someone or something through the eyes of wanting or judging. Rather, you see as if you were seeing in a mirror. The person whom you used to see as an object is now the subject, the same as you. You see the reflection equal to you, no less, no more. The reflection is not different from what you are.

Once there was an artist. He decided to put pieces of mirror all around his room, on the ceiling and on the walls, so that they would reflect the one light which was in his room. And it was his joy to sit and watch the reflected lights. By chance his dog entered the room. Not being able to understand that the dogs he saw in the mirrors were his own reflections, he started barking at what he viewed as rivals. He saw so many other dogs, and he could not stop barking. Eventually he became exhausted and collapsed. The poor dog saw the many reflections only as rivals biting and jumping at him. In this way, he created duality.

See the world as a reflection of your own desires. Remove your desires and only see. Do not bark. When you see yourself as the seer, the world merges in your awareness.

This is one insight. It is difficult to explain, but when you feel it, it makes you equal to all. Then it does not make any difference to you if you are with a rich man or a poor man, a prince or a pauper. It does not create any fluctuation in your mind. Why not? Because you now have a new perception. What you see in you is in him. His "I" and your "I" are the same in quality, pure *Atma.*

If you see in terms of "less" and "more," then you will see a common man as less and a friend with a high post as more. When you see another as object instead of subject, he who has more things is seen as a rich object and he who has fewer things is seen as a poor object. This kind of relationship, which we notice so often, is an objective relationship. And that kind of relationship is maintained only so long as certain things are there. When those things are no longer there, the relationship is over. Why? Because the dependency in the relationship is on outside things.

This reflection brings a new way of thinking. Starting with yourself, say, "*Ekatva,* I am One. I came as One into the world. Traveling alone and floating from the universe, I entered some sweet mother's womb and there I rested to grow."

In this way you go beyond and see how you came alone. At that time nobody knew you. You were a stranger. You did not have any address, acquaintance, or letter of recommendation. You had nothing.

All of us came alone in a small vehicle, in a microscopic form—a sperm and egg. At that time we had no equipment. Now we have so much equipment with which to see, express, speak, and move. But at the outset of this life, we entered in a small body, our vehicle. That's all!

At that time who was there? For whom were you crying? Now you are crying for so many things, but then you were crying for one—to take a deep breath! That was your first need. You cried, you breathed, and all the body processes started working. The first thing you could feel was the heart beating.

Go on working with the thought, "I came as One," and you will know how to stand on your own feet. Tears handicap your vision when you cry, "I can't live without you! I can't live without this or that!" It is all mental addiction. You have lived without them! You came alone! At that time you wanted only breath and something to sustain the body. So you can live without them now!

The idea behind this meditation is to make an individual strong to stand on his or her own. In this way, the person will not lean on anyone or become a burden to someone. The point is not to separate you from the world, but to make you a healthy person. When you build your inner muscles, your mind becomes sound and vigorous. You realize you *can* be alone.

From the moment you came into the world, you started unfolding that invisible through the visible. Human life is nothing but an unfolding of the invisible. And the unfolding brings out so many qualities.

Take the seed of any plant. It is so insignificant-looking. When it unfolds, sprouts up, and brings out a beautiful flower, then we realize that that beauty was hidden in that tiny yellow, white, or black seed. At the beginning, we do not pay much attention to the seed, but when the seed uncovers its whole beauty, we notice it. In the same way, this invisible soul has had from beginningless time all this beauty. Now it is unfolding through human life.

According to the seed, the form is created. The quality of the seed determines the result, its blossoming. That is why, if we have the seed of a rose, then a rose flower comes. If we plant the seed of a mango, the seed will open its heart and turn into a delicious mango. When an apple seed grows, apples come. But you don't see the apples and mangoes when you first look at those small black seeds. Yet in your awareness, you can know that they hold unique qualities.

So meditate on that tiny beginning of yours. Go back and see, "I came alone, there was joy, no fear, no addiction."

You will be surprised to know that the more addictions you have, the sooner old age comes. The fewer addictions, the more youthful you remain. People wither because of their tensions and worries.

Watch yourself when you are on a vacation. You feel fresh. Why? You don't have any demands, any pulls. Demands and addictions corrode you. You think you are getting something by continuing with them, but really you are decaying inside.

That is why wise people don't have addictions to so many things. Once there was a wise man who lived in a big house. But his house was empty. One evening, some thieves came. "What to do?" the wise man thought.

"Thieves don't have any sense, and when they find out that I don't have anything for them to take, they will be angry. They may try to harm me."

So he opened his only cupboard, which was empty, and hid himself inside. The thieves came and looked about. They found nothing. When they noticed the cupboard, they opened it. They saw the old man standing there.

"Why are you hiding yourself from us?" they asked.

"What to answer?" he thought. Then he said, "I am hiding from you because of shame."

"What is your shame?" they asked him.

"Sirs," he answered, "there is nothing in this house to present to you. I am ashamed to have nothing to offer to you guests. So I thought I must hide."

The thieves laughed. "Yes," they said, "you are a wise man because you don't have anything."

"Yes," answered the wise man, "if you have something, you have worry. If you don't have anything, what worry can you have?"

By collecting things, you are collecting worries. You even worry whether or not people notice what you have. If guests come and do not appreciate your painting, you think they don't have any sense of appreciation. If thieves come and take it away, you also fret.

The initiate is given this reflection so that he will not become unhappy upon seeing so many worldly things. As a monk, he goes from house to house for his alms. At that time, he should not become upset that he has nothing in his monastery except four walls and an empty room. So he meditates on that oneness.

"I came into the world with nothing, only my good vibrations. Because of them, I have been unfolding my human life. Identifying with so many material things, I am getting tired, exhausted, withered. I don't want to carry this burden on my head any more."

At the same time, the initiate meditates on the exit he or she is going to make from this world. "I came alone and I will go alone."

It is the truth. It may make you feel sad. Always when some created illusion drops away, there is sadness unless you see the truth behind it. Then you become happy. The heart may cry for what it has lost, but the soul laughs for what it has gained!

So we enter and exit alone. Then why do we live with the world? What is this whole human family? Why do we have friends? If we come and go alone, why do we need this whole thing?

There is a meaning. *We are here to communicate, to build a bridge with the world, but not to bind ourselves to the world.* This is the difference. A bridge allows us to go from one end to another. Bondage ties us to one end and does not allow us to go anywhere. Knowing this, we use the process of bridging rather than that of binding.

However, our mental habit is inclined toward addiction and binding. We always want to bind things to ourselves. Once George Bernard Shaw was sitting by a window overlooking his garden. His cousin went into the garden, plucked many flowers, and put them in a vase. Shaw asked him, "Why did you do this?"

His cousin answered, "To decorate our drawing room."

So Shaw asked, "If somebody came and cut off your head, how would you feel? Why did you not go into the garden and enjoy the blossoming plants? I sit and watch from here. To decorate the house, you had to take them out from their own place. Why do you not go to them instead?"

It is an example of the psychology of the mind. When you have attachment, you don't want to see life grow in its own place. You want to keep it, put it in a packet, affix your label to it, and call it your own. You want to say, "It belongs to me." If you do this, what happens? The life soon withers.

When this insight opens and blossoms, you become very comfortable with the world. You are friends with all. You say, "Let us be as bridges and communicate with one another."

You no longer care to be a cause for bondage to anybody. You want to be free, not tied down. If you identify with a person in a binding way, taking his or her problem on your head, then you are not giving space. You will become irritated when the person does not do as you desire. You will complain, "He is not doing as I wish. I have told him twenty times and still he does not listen." You become unhappy, angry. Why? Because you identify.

If you are building a bridge with your friend, you say what you feel, and if your friend does not agree, at least you can say, "We agree that we don't agree." There also you have agreement. There is no reason to be angry. It's a very subtle feeling—to untie yourself from all the ties.

We have not come into the world to fight, to quarrel, to be sad, and in the evening to go to bed miserable. We are not here in the world for that. There are many who are engaged in such vicious, circular behavior. Let them do it. Those whose minds are obsessed with worldly things—power, position, money—cannot do otherwise! And you can notice what happens to them when their power and worldly attachments go; their life sinks very low. You cannot imagine their bitterness, their sorrow. But it is the nature of those things to go. People become sad because they allow their whole mind and energy to be consumed by those things which ultimately have to go.

But you, who want to grow and help others grow, know that this life is to build communication. You tell yourself, "Let me commune with as many people as possible." And your relationships are genuine because you are not creating duality.

A person may be short or tall, thin or fat, rich or poor, of one race or another, educated or not; you relate to the subject who is in the center of that person. You don't consider anyone as higher or lower. You do not limit yourself by that kind of fluctuation. So any fluctuation which is causing anxiety goes away and from that moment you have a very fine connection with the world. It becomes easy to move and communicate with all, because you are with people on a level of sharing.

When one meditates on aloneness, there is the possibility of fear creeping in. "I am alone? Is there nobody in the whole world whom I can call mine?" you might think. That thought may frighten you and make you feel gloomy.

When this occurs, you must see yourself in a new way. See yourself as an individual, as a life force. In your meditation see the dynamic, potent reality of your Self. As you focus on this energy, you will realize that you are eternal, the creator of your future. In the ancient teachings, we call it the *simhavruti,* the quality of lionhood.

The lion in the forest does not move in big herds. In a zoo you may see several lions together, but not in a wild forest. There each lion has his own abode, his own cave, his own kingdom. A lion wants to be alone. At the same time, he does not have any fear in his heart. He knows he is the king. That lionhood must emerge in meditation. That fearlessness must be experienced.

Once a lioness was killed and her small cub went wandering in the wilderness. A shepherd found him and took him home. He reared the cub with his own goats and sheep. The cub grew up with them, growing bigger and stronger each day.

One day all the sheep and goats, along with this lion cub, were grazing when a big lion came to the top of the mountain above their meadow and roared with all his might. Hearing the roar, all the sheep, goats, and the little cub started running away. The lion who roared saw them all run and thought, "Yes, they all must run, but why is that lion cub running away also?"

He ran after the cub and grabbed him. The cub became frightened and began bleating. So the lion drew him near the water and said, "Why do you bleat? You are a lion! Look at your reflection in the water and roar." But the little lion did not understand or believe his words. He wandered off to graze.

"What are you doing, nibbling blades of grass?" asked the great lion. "This is not your food." By this time the lion cub was trembling.

"Why are you trembling?" he asked the baby cub. "I am like you. You are like me. You have forgotten your nature."

This mind is so weak that once it has accepted a certain form, it is difficult to convince it of another approach. It remains in the same frame, the same compartment. Our mind limits itself in this way. The lion cub was not ready to leave his limited way of seeing. But the big lion would not rest until he had convinced him.

"No, you must understand," he told him. "You are like me."

He made him look into the water of the pond. He stood beside him and said, "See your reflection. See my reflection. See your yellow color, your mane, your tail. See how curly it is. See your sharp teeth just like mine. See your lion face." And the cub started seeing and thinking.

"Yes, I have a big lion face. It is true. I'm not covered with fleece and I don't have horns on my head. Yes, but this animal roars and I say 'Baa, baa.' It's a big difference!"

"Well, young lion, bring out your voice! Your heart is very large. I can hear its throbs, so bring your roaring voice out!"

The cub tried a little bit. He opened his throat, but because of habit, his voice box was contracted and he could not roar. Slowly he made an effort and at last the real roar came out.

"Now," the great lion told him, "walk alone. Don't move in the herd. You do not belong there. They are all sheep and goats. You are a lion. How can you live with sheep and goats? Now go there and make a roar!"

So the cub went back and roared so fiercely that they all ran away, sheep, goats, shepherd, and all. He realized his nature. He was transformed. "I am able to stand alone. At the same time, I can live without feelings of helplessness and fear."

So *ekatva* is a transforming reflection. It gives a new ideal, a new perception to your mind. Slowly this becomes a symbol and you start seeing yourself in another dimension.

"I come alone and I go alone, but I am not alone.

Knowing that oneness in me, I see it in each individual. So all are like me and I am like all."

You have respect for all, as you have respect for yourself. You are neither superior nor inferior. Both scales have gone. You are one with all. When you treat everyone as equal, each person feels comfortable with you. If you treat someone as inferior, he may feel resentful or unsure of himself. If you treat someone as superior, he may feel uncomfortable also. He won't know how to be with you. He is no greater than you, but by your making him great, he may try to hide his smallness and live up to your false image of him.

We are on an eternal journey. From here, do we have an itinerary? Most cannot say, but we do know that all must go somewhere. That's the law of the universe.

Where do we go? We go to those places, to those people, to those conditions which we are preparing here and now with our love, our connection, our bridgebuilding between each other. What we are creating now will be waiting to greet us then. It may sound a little paradoxical. But when you go deeper and deeper through meditation into your timeless infinite being, you touch your life's quest. That becomes your invisible path. That becomes your dream come true. That becomes your eternal journey into evolution.

Each person is an individual traveler. At the same time, he is in company. We have both, individuality and company. In a subtle sense, it is oneness; in a general sense, it is allness. In one way, it is the invisible world; in another way, it is this visible world. The two are deeply interconnected, working together on a personal level as well as on a universal plane to bring a soul to its ultimate fruition.

From now on, you can start working with the world on a universal level. Notice if you are seeing a person as an object or as a subject. It is a daily practice. Start from today. Ask yourself, "How do I see that person?" First create a mental picture. Do you see him or her exactly equal to you? When you do, then tell yourself, "What I don't like, that person may not like, so I must not do that. And what I want, that person may want. So let me share and give space, live and let live."

When you experience oneness, you have won your goal in life. When you don't see that oneness, then you are constantly dependent, always crying on somebody's shoulder. What happens when you don't find a shoulder to cry on? You are miserable. But if you build inner strength and understanding, then, even in old age, you will have friends around you. They will feel neither burdened nor bound by you; they will enjoy communication with you, subject to subject.

This unique meditation helps us have a glimpse of the truth. It allows us to see that the flame in our being is the same flame everywhere. The outer shapes may be different—the chimneys, the bulbs, the shades—but inside, the living light is the same. You become aware of everyone as flame, including yourself. Only on this level is a bridge of communication built. There is no other way to build such a bridge with mankind. So long as you see forms, there is no bridge.

In realizing that everyone has this quality of light, you discover that it is inborn, not given or applied. It is man's intrinsic nature, his birthright as a human being. That is why this teaching has great relevance to our lives. It removes the old habit of the mind which likes to create duality and it brings our lionhood to the surface. When the mind starts to separate, saying, "Somebody else has this quality of lion, not I," remember *ekatva* to bring you back to yourself. Experience the oneness. See the lion quality in yourself as well as in others.

Now you are ready to know both, your innate potentiality and your present condition, your center and your circumference. By meditating on the multiple and the solitary, you can remove the manyness, peel away the layers of mind, and bring out that exultant feeling of all-oneness.

Seed-Thoughts for Meditation

Ekatva, *I am One. I came alone into the world. I will depart alone. I know how to stand alone, without addiction or prop, apart from the herd, fearless and strong in my Self.*

I have only to go into the depth of aloneness to know the meaning of all-oneness.

Everyone has come into the world to know this oneness, to build a bridge of communication with one another.

Let me be aware of everyone as flame, as living light, including myself. Let me realize the magnificence and potency of soul and become universal.

FACET FIVE

In Search of the Incomparable

HUMAN life is a place where we can grow in peace and understanding, provided we get some light. Without light, this place can be chaos and we can get lost in it. Like traveling at night without a torch in hand, we may stumble and tumble down anywhere.

Human life is engulfed in beauty and mystery. It is overwhelming. It overpowers us and thrills us. The mind tries to explore it, peep into it, get to the heart of it. It cannot succeed. It is like a child trying to tell about the vastness of the ocean by expanding his arms as he cries out, "I saw so much water! It was so-o-o big!" His expression does not come close to describing the vastness of the ocean. In the same way, when the mind tries to describe the mystery of this universe, it is like a child. The mind cannot reveal or comprehend it. Why? Because the mystery of the living universe is unlimited and the mind is limited.

So we need some light, some power which is beyond the mind, which is unlimited. When we have that kind of light, then we are able to comprehend the universal mystery. Then we are able to educate the mind and loosen its hold on concepts, forms, and definitions. If we do not enlighten our mind, then it will assume the role of teacher; and though the unenlightened mind is nothing but a child in primary school, it will pretend to explain all the secrets of the universe.

If we allow ourselves to be guided by this limited mind, two things will happen. Outside we will not know how to relate, and inside we will not know how to live in peace. Outside, our relationships will be spoiled or disturbed, and inside there will be constant upheaval or conflict. From these come frustration and friction.

So we see our need for some light. From where does the light come? From deep inner experience, from meditating on those experiences which have come from the masters to the initiates. Such a light can help us see subjectively the inner conflict and objectively the outside confusion.

But to understand and experience the experiences of the masters, we need some preparation, some groundwork. The vessel must be ready to receive the force of the essence which is poured into it. If it is not, the vessel will be broken or destroyed or melted, and the essence will be lost in the dust. In the same way, if our mind is not prepared for the truth, it may become frightened and be unable to bear the truth.

So the initiates ready themselves to receive inside truth. They strengthen their vessel to be in accordance with the essence. That is why they digest and assimilate the teaching into their lives. That is why they find peace in life. In this world, they are able to live with such an awareness that they neither misuse their energy nor experience conflict. They do not inflict pain, sadness, or torture on themselves or on others.

Generally, those people who you think are intellectual and skillful in the world are not what they seem to be on the surface. If you watch them with a balanced mind, in a nonjudgmental way, you will see that they are doing nothing but inculcating pain in their life. There comes a point when there is so much sorrow and pain that they are not able to bear it. So they take many things to cover it up and soothe it. They take medicine to tranquilize the pain. Tranquilizers indicate that man is inflicting pain on himself. To relieve or minimize the effect of the pain, he resorts to many outer things: wine, drugs, pills; or he runs after pleasure and sense gratification. They all indicate that underneath there is some pain.

If you can develop insight, at least you will not inflict pain on your own self. You won't have to be in that parade. By not joining the procession, at least you will be in a position to help other people who need your help. If you are driven by the current of the parade, then your feet are marching to the beat of someone else's drum. You are not moving according to your own pace.

First you have to stand back and watch the parade without becoming involved with the march or the music. You take these reflections to help remove yourself from the crowd. Use them to come out from the world of make-believe and see reality as it is. It may be painful. You are not used to seeing in that way. You are used to living in a world of fantasy. But without clarity, how can you go further?

The last facet was *ekatva*—to meditate on that indestructible energy that is you. Unless you get in touch with that, you will not be able to free yourself from all the fears. Unless you experience your aloneness, you will not be able to realize oneness.

Today is the day to focus on the fifth facet—*anyatva-swatva. Anyatva* means that which is other than your essence or Self. *Swatva* means Selfhood. It helps you to see two things: 1) *anya,* where you have mistakenly identified yourself or mixed yourself up, and 2) *swa,* your real Self.

It is a process of separation. You are not that with which you have identified. Your real Self cannot be identified with anything. It is unique.

Ask yourself, "What are those things with which I have identified?" You can know what they are by observing your reaction when you are required to live without them. If you have created identity with something, and that something is taken away from you, you experience great pain. In that loss you feel loss. In its destruction you feel destruction. In its decay you feel decay. In every dependency you are inviting pain.

Observe what happens when you identify with something. You turn it into an idea. Then you become a prisoner of the created idea. You want to maintain it at all costs. And that is what people do. They kill for an idea. Not only that, they die for it. All the isms, patriotism, sectarianism, dogmatism, are nothing but a camouflage for self-punishment. Holding onto ideas, we punish ourselves. But we have not come into the world to punish ourselves. We are not here to be angry and separate from other human beings. Being angry, we hurt ourselves. The idea behind this philosophy is to be free from pain, to be healthy.

So contemplate how many things you have bound yourself to: racial, cultural, or religious labels, possessions, sensory objects, relatives and friends. See that by holding onto them, instead you are caught. By trying to make them yours, you become a prisoner to them. Stop punishing yourself. Disidentify, untie, and free! Why create attachment to things which are on the road to decay? Ultimately they depart from us or we depart from them. When this happens, there is inner pain. Why? Because identifying with them, we keep them deep down in our subconscious, and when they go along with the process of nature, our clinging mind feels the loss.

To transcend all forms of self-punishment, know your incomparable Self. Experience the difference between what is Self and what is not, and see that what is yours can never be taken away from you, and that what is not yours never can be owned.

Take this insight into your meditation on your relationships. For example, you may have built a relationship with a particular man. When you see him talking to another woman, there is a burning sensation, an uncomfortable feeling. Why? What has gone? Nothing has gone. But your mind has built an identity with that person, and because of its attachment to "mine," it feels threatened and in pain. If you did not build identity with that person, seeing him with someone else would not bother you. You would not care. But when the mind is spying, it is constantly engaged. It is thinking, "Why does he meet with her? What is his intention?" So long as the mind is spying in that way, do you think you will be able to meditate and think of divinity?

Moreover, if you are not able to free yourself from that burning sensation, and if it lasts for three or four days, it will create indigestion. To digest food, the whole body needs a pleasant, relaxed flow of energy. When you are tense, the body cells are contracted. Where there is contraction, there is no digestion. Constipation indicates that inside we are burning with unhappiness. The burning energy absorbs all our digestive juices. People don't see how much energy they are burning up in jealousy, in spying, in thinking "mine" and "thine."

The word "agony" comes from the Sanskrit *agni,* or fire, and later, from the Greek *agou,* or struggle. Jealousy is both, a fire and a struggle. It burns! When you are completely roasted and toasted inside, the juice is gone! Agony comes when people create an attachment for each other's bodies. See what happens when there is a separation or divorce. People break with difficulty. They say, "She has spoiled my life," or "He has spoiled my life." No one has spoiled your life except you with your own thoughts.

In reflecting on *anyatva,* start with your own body and say, "The body is different from what I am. The body is *anya,* or other. I am *swa,* or Self." Don't confuse one with the other. See them for what they are. When you stop mixing them up, you will be able to know what it is to have companionship. You will know, "What is living, sentient, and formless is ever-moving energy; that is me. What is composing and decomposing is insentient energy. That is the body." The first is neither composing nor decomposing; the second is always composing and decomposing.

Our bodies are conceived from a single cell. The formation of the body is a process of cells dividing from one to two, from two to four, from four to eight, and so on. The body increases its weight every day. Eight or nine pounds of weight have come from one single cell multiplying, composing, and decomposing. There is not a single moment in which the process stops. It goes on until the last day of our lives.

When we meditate on that, we see the process in its entirety. At any time, that which is composed can decompose. It is not a new discovery. There is no reason for it to give you a shock. When you understand it, you are no longer surprised by anything. The unknown surprises you, but the known is a fact, a statement. You accept it.

Separating yourself through meditation from this process of composing and decomposing, you then ask, "Who is animating this process? Who is beyond this process?" You answer, "That is I." "I" sits there in the center. This must become your experience, as clear as the day. Then you will know you have experienced a spiritual glimpse. You will realize, "I am that which is not destructible. I am that which remains unchanged. It is the outside which goes on changing."

Go further and observe, "This body is nothing but a reflection of my inside perception." A person who goes on thinking in an ugly way builds an ugly body. A person who thinks beautifully builds a beautiful body. If you feel rage and bitterness toward someone, it will be seen on your face. If you were to set up an automatic camera to take your own picture every time you felt rage, you would not want to recognize yourself.

Faces are neither young nor old; it is inside perception which changes them. There are young people whose faces are cruel, and there are old people whose faces are mellow, molded with compassion. An angry face takes a tense form. It is distorted. A peaceful face takes a poised form, due to an inside composed feeling. The world is not agony or pain. Pain is your own confusion. The world is neutral. You can make what you want out of it.

So now we see that the condition of the body is the result of yesterday's perception. There is no need to blame anybody else. There is the body and there is the Self. The Self is that which animates the body. Our body is not at fault for the way it looks. By feeling an inside feeling of health, pleasantness, love, we are slowly changing our form with our thoughts. These thoughts are formed inside and the result will ultimately show on the outside.

Watch the outer world and experience the inner world. In this way, you will know the two are complementary to each other. Live with pure joy in the body; keep it clean, beautiful, relaxed, and wholesome. This vehicle is not for any masochistic purpose. The real ascetic is he or she who does not destroy this beautiful vehicle. Ignorant people torture their body instead of changing their perception. They punish it as though the body were the cause of their suffering. They do not see that the body can be at their command. It is inside perception which must be changed.

That is why one of the basic steps is called *shaucha*—cleanliness. Keep your body and mind clean and you will go toward godliness. Someone with a dirty body, unclean mouth, ill-smelling clothes is not headed for salvation. The body must first be healthy and clean. See that your energy can be felt through all the pores.

See that you are clean emotionally. Remove bad intentions from your consciousness. Don't encourage gossip. Don't misuse your hands; use them for service.

When you eat, be in tune with your food. The monks observe silence while eating, and say to themselves, "Oh Lord! Through awareness of you, I realize that this body is a means to liberation. So with innocent and sanctified food, I nourish this body in order to reach the goal." Keeping this in mind, you make your body a beautiful and useful vehicle for your growth. You see it for what it is.

Observe: "I am not that which I am using. My possessions are for my best use, growth, progress, and communication." When anything comes, you give room to it. When it goes, you let it pass by, float by. There is no need to lower your horns and fight for something like a bull!

Those people who want to be with you, let them be with you! To those who don't want to be with you, say, "Goodbye now!" When they come again, say, "Welcome!" Do not live on past revenge or vindictiveness. If something has gone or is going, let it go! In this way, you become so free.

Ultimately, everything is going to go. It is easy to talk about it, but difficult to live it. When the moment comes in which we are tested, sometimes we act differently. Why does a dog love a piece of bone? It has no juice, no meat. It has nothing. It is dry. But the dog goes on chewing on it, and in the process of chewing sometimes cuts its own palate. It bleeds, and the blood gets on the bone. The dog licks it and thinks, "Oh, the sweetness!" Pleasure is so sweet to it that it forgets the whole process of pain. Clinging to things is a habit of the mind. The initiates see material things for what they are, without coloring or creating distortion. When you see clearly, you don't suffer objective conflict or subjective confusion. You are free from both.

When you meditate on *swatva,* you slowly begin to feel that what you are is not comparable with any worldly thing. Say to yourself, "I am living with living energy." Whenever and wherever you see living energy, you feel the flow of love with those living beings.

When you see other human beings, see the soul in them. As you have seen the "I am" in yourself, you see the "I am" in them. In this way, you will not live on an attachment level. You will not try to possess people and put them in your "purse." Let them be what they are. Live on a love level, not on a possession level.

If you are genuine, others will be genuine. If you don't see a genuine relationship growing, then let the person go on his or her way. Say to yourself, "I am not here to take on anybody's pain." See how smooth and pleasant and loving your relationships will become, because you are not creating suffocation. There is no binding; rather, it is genuine communication of life to life.

Knowing your reality, you will see that reality in all living forms. Then you will know the meaning of compassion. Compassion is not seeing the form of human, plant, or animal; it is seeing the life. Once Abraham Lincoln saw a pig stuck in the mud. He told his driver to stop the carriage. He got down into the mud and pulled the pig out. He lost concern for his dress clothes. He transcended the form and saw the pain of life.

Compassion is saying to yourself, "If I were in that condition, how would I feel?" So when you see pain, your heart flies there to elevate life from its burden. In this way, you come out from the old habit of identifying life with form; instead, see form as nothing but the externalization of inner life.

You also begin to see that nothing is permanent in this world of forms—of things and emotions and thoughts. You may think you have "urgent" work to do, but when you look very deeply, there is nothing you can call a lifetime mission except to live and to grow. In Rajkot, there was a police officer who made an appointment with me. He had something he wanted to talk about with me. As monks, we had the duty of complying with someone's request if we had free time to do so. I was a little busy, so I suggested we meet the next morning. He said, "I would be glad to make it tomorrow, but I have very urgent work tomorrow. I am expected to attend a big case in court. Please let us meet today." So we agreed to meet at 4 P.M.

A few hours later, a fellow monk came to me and said, "The police officer has expired." He thought he had a big case to attend the next morning, but life's mission had changed the date for him.

So what is your lifetime mission? To live day by day, to identify with life and to go to bed each night with love for all, ill will for none. There is no dead end for you. Your life will go on creating. When you think, "Leaving this experience, I will continue evolving elsewhere," your compulsion and hurry will drop away. You will live and grow in beautiful relationships each day, with yourself and with all living life.

☙ Seed-Thoughts for Meditation

Let me see that I am Self, and that I have misidentified myself with that which is other than Self.

I have allowed my limited mind to identify with ephemeral things and turn them into concepts. Binding myself to them, I have become bound. Now I turn to that light which is beyond mind and vaster than the material world. In throwing that light on the octopus grip of the mind, I can persuade it to loosen its hold. I want to free myself of dependency and perceive life clearly. I want to experience the beauty of my incomparable Self.

The world is not agony or pain. Pain is my own confusion, my own possessiveness. The world is neutral. I am now going to use it as a testing ground for my growth, as an inspiration for my progress, as a means to take me closer to all living life.

FACET SIX

The Flame in the Candle

ANYONE who is in a hypnotic trance or under a spell is not going to act according to his own will. Why not? Because his will has been subdued. It has been subjected to someone else's command, to the suggestion of the hypnotist. So the person performs an action, but does not know why he is doing it. When you observe him, you cannot tell whether his action comes from his own free will or from some suggestion.

This same thing happens in our own lives. The way we move, dress, eat, communicate, think, and act is another kind of spell. We go through various motions. We engage in a number of activities. But do we know whether our action comes from self-awareness or from someone else's suggestion? Can we detect whether we are acting according to a subtle "brainwash" created by society, politics, religion, business, the world of "isms"? Have we assimilated and internalized the influences of the outside world to such an extent that our thoughts, desires, likes and dislikes, actions and reactions are under their spell? Or are our lives flowing from our own will, our own self-awareness?

We may not be able to differentiate between the outer influence and our own desire. We may not be able to isolate the factors which are coloring our ways of thinking and living. So we keep on doing the same thing. We continue to tread the same path, deepen the same rut, follow the same routine.

That is why we need meditation. *Meditation is a process to dehypnotize the human consciousness.* This is the heart of the teaching. Mind, body, and senses are all hypnotized. We need to dehypnotize them. We need to learn how to stand back and see.

It is not an easy task. Without standing back and becoming a keen but dispassionate observer, we cannot detect the ways in which the mind, body, and senses are en-tranced. Why is it so difficult? Because it is mass hypnotism. Society influences in two ways: from mass values and from sheer numbers. When the masses do something, it has a hypnotic effect on the individual. For example, if ten people are dancing and you are alone in a corner of the same room, even if you do not intend to dance, you will feel like getting up to dance. If ten people are in a room meditating and you come in intending to dance, you will not dance. Even if the individual is strong, societal influence ultimately takes over in the majority of cases. So mass values and customs influence the minority and are perpetuated by the majority.

The *bhavanas* are for the seekers who are from different backgrounds and of a wide range of mental, emotional, and physical habits and patterns. They have not yet freed themselves from the spell of mass hypnotism. These reflections are to free them from the spell. The primary purpose of this teaching is to liberate the human consciousness.

In the sixth reflection, we distinguish between two elements—*suchi,* the ascending, and *asuchi,* the descending. We observe these two urges in us. Like the candle, we have something constantly moving upward. We can call it the flame. We have another something melting downward. It is the wax. These two have their own distinct natures.

What is moving upward? It is our longing to find something pure and beautiful, something high and noble, something subtle and divine. Each one of us has this quest. That is why we are called aspirants, or *sadhaka,* meaning not complacent. We want each step to find us farther than the last.

The dream you had ten years ago may have been realized by now. You find that you want something more. You want to go further. This "more" is the nature of that upward-moving element. Wherever you go and whatever you receive, that "more" is there. It will remain till the last, till you reach the best. You have not reached the height yet; that is why that longing is there.

So meditate on *suchi* and ask yourself, "What is moving upward in me? What is the pure, unique essence of life? Let me not confuse that with other elements which are composing and decomposing."

Investigate, "What is the quality of my thoughts and emotions? What is the frequency of my vibrations? Are they lifting me up or taking me down? Are they increasing the heaviness in me, or are they focused on revealing my light?"

It is very important to have a sense of discrimination to differentiate between these two. Without this discriminating sense, we run the risk of identifying our pure essence with the matter-laden coverings weighing it down. Without the light of awareness, the mind deludes us. That is the influence of the hypnotic spell. We allow ourselves to live without the experience of who we really are. This is self-deception. There is no outside deceiver who can fool you more than your own inaccurate thinking. You may think, "I have everything. I can buy anything I want. I am happy." But unexpectedly sorrow creeps in and all of a sudden your mood is depressed.

So we take a little time to investigate our inertia, the heaviness which does not allow us to move. We see clearly what is covered with shadow, sorrow, and heavy desires. Otherwise, the negative vibrations which are the substance of those gravitating tendencies in us will continue to attract karmas or particles of matter to us and obscure our vision. As long as we allow our thoughts to run wild and unchecked, our mind will be subjected to the continuing influx of these undesirable elements.

Rather than suppress your thoughts, watch them. Do you want to overcome sorrow and guilt? Then observe the way in which sorrow works. Notice how it has a way of waiting in the corner a little distance away and then how it tackles you all of a sudden without giving you a chance to think. Your discriminatory sense itself tends to get covered. One minute you were blossoming with a smile, the next minute you are sad and morose. What has happened? Where has your happiness gone? Where was this depressed mood waiting? It was waiting in the mind.

Once sorrow invades you, you have no strength to overcome it. You sink lower and lower. You might have noticed that when you are under the clouds of sadness, even if you recite a *mantra* and pray, you are sometimes not able to lift yourself out of that feeling. In those moments, where is all the wisdom? It remains in a corner. Though our heads are filled with a lot of quotations, do we use them when we are under the influence of sorrow? We do not. Though we have read books on how to be happy, do they help us? Apparently not. It seems that we are only able to use their wisdom when we are in a good mood. It is most important that we learn to call upon our knowledge and insights to sustain us when we are in a low state. We must remember them, call them forth, and put them to use.

Why don't we use our knowledge? Because intellectual information and emotional feeling work in different directions. For example, intellectually we know that anyone who comes into our life is eventually going to go. We are aware that all are on a journey, coming and going, but when that event happens in our life, how do we take it? Intellectually we understand, but emotionally what is our reaction? Meditation helps us bring that knowledge into our feeling. Experiencing our feeling, we change our perception. Changing our perception, we become ready to meet any challenge. Nothing comes as a shock or a surprise. Understanding has been absorbed into our experience.

The wise person lives in the world, but not of it. He lives with complete awareness. There is a zen story which illustrates this. Once there was a famous swordsman who was on his deathbed when his son asked him, "What is your last wish, father?"

His father answered, "Oh, Matajura, my son, I had a dream to see you become the greatest of swordsmen, but I failed."

Matajura told him, "And I also wanted to become that, but the right teacher could not be found, and you also had no time to teach me."

Then his father said, "This wish is so strong that I am going to live three more years to see that it is fulfilled. Though I am on my deathbed, I shall not die."

So his son asked, "Who shall be my teacher?" His father sent him to Banzo, who was known to be the master at that time.

The boy went to Banzo and bowed and said, "I want

to study with you and become a skilled swordsman. I am willing to devote myself completely to this task. How long will it take for me to master the art?"

The master answered, "Twelve years."

"Twelve years?" The boy was incredulous. "Suppose I use every moment of my day and allow for only three hours' sleep, then how long will it take?"

"Then it may take twenty years!" The boy did not understand.

So the master explained, "One who is in haste and keeps his eye only on the result and not on the process gets no result. I teach not for result but for life. Master swordsmanship means to be vigilant, to know how not to kill and yet how to protect oneself. You must know that in the sword there is no friendly edge. If I teach only for result, you will be sliced. What for? I care more for the welfare of your life."

Now the boy understood. He told the master, "Sir, I drop the idea of timing. I request that you accept me as your student. I will become a vessel to receive wisdom from you."

From that day, he was accepted as the master's student. Now that his mind was calm, he was to receive a special training in awareness. The first part of the training was to do many kinds of service for his teacher. He washed his clothes, gardened, prepared food for him, kept the swords in order, and took care of many other things. In six months, he was not given a single moment to learn how to hold or use the sword, but he had patience.

One day while he was gardening, his teacher came and hit him with a wooden sword. He told him, "From today I will come unexpectedly. If you are aware, I will not hit you. If you are not aware, I will strike you. Harder blows are to come."

"Yes, sir," the student answered. He was very serious and eager to learn. He knew, "My teacher is harsh in appearance but soft in feeling. I don't know why he is hurting me, but he must have some good intention."

Soon the student began to be ready for a blow to come from any direction and at any time. Before the teacher came, he would know it. In this way, he became constantly alert and prepared for anything. As soon as the master put his hand on his sheath, the student would become aware and look up at him.

After that, his teacher told him, "Now starts the second part of your training. I will come at night. If you do not awaken, I will hit you." Each night the student would know even before the teacher appeared. Day and night he was alert. He became a body with no desires. His whole being was nothing but vigilance.

After two years, one night the master came not to hit him, but to smile at him and praise him. "Now you are the best swordsman!"

"But you have not taught me!" protested his student.

"To practice the sword is not a big thing," the master explained. "I can teach you that in a short time, but to be aware of which direction the sword is coming from, that is the main thing. To be vigilant, that is greatness. To overcome impulses, habits, lethargy, and inertia, that is real mastery. Now go anywhere in the world. Nothing will cover you, for even deep sleep does not make you slumber. My mission to teach you is over. It was to make you aware."

In life, events come, vibrations hit us, karmas from the past give us blows. If we are not aware, they can throw us off balance. But if we are aware, we meet them as challenges. We meet them with the infinite source of strength hidden within us. We must come to know that strength. How do we come to know it? Through awareness of life. Our awareness must be built on reverence for life. Then, all actions are directed from that reverence.

Nothing fetters or binds the person who is aware. Working, sleeping, eating, communicating, you are aware of everything you do as an act of reverence and love, honoring the one within who knows and is vigilant. Then whatever you do is for your growth and freedom. You do it without becoming attached or identified with the action. You see that your motive is pure, just to be, just to evolve, just to live and help others to live. In this way, you free yourself from the spell of greed and other mass values, and you feel the power and joy of self-mastery.

We have seen how the unaware mind allows heavy vibrations such as sorrow to invade it and act as a gravitating influence in our life. Now we are going to consider the meaning of *asuchi* in another way. The body itself is *asuchi;* that is, its nature is to decompose. Ultimately, all the cells of the body disintegrate, and the components or elements return to a simpler form.

What are the elements of the body? The ancients referred to them as earth, water, fire, and air. For instance, teeth and nails relate to the earth element; blood and saliva to the water element; body heat and the nervous system to the fire element; and breath to the air element. These four elements constitute each human form. They are the same everywhere. According to the particles of our past thoughts, emotions, words, and deeds, which we call karmas, the elements take on different shapes and colors. Innumerable designs and unique kaleidoscopic patterns are seen, but the constituents do not change. In each body they remain the same earth, the same water, the same fire, and the same air.

How is it that these four elements take on so many different forms? The answer lies in the law of vibrations. Each and every action of your life sends out vibrations that attract those physical elements from the universe which will form the body accordingly. In this way, your thinking, living, and doing create different forms and colors from the basic elements of earth, water, fire, and air. The differences in individuals reflect the innumerable differences in people's intentions, feelings, and living patterns.

Becoming aware of this law of vibrations, you have no need to feel guilty or sad. You begin to observe with balance the causes and effects in your life and, at the same time, you stop blaming others for the way you are. You eliminate the habit of false pride as well as the habit of false humility, both of which occur from ignorance of Self. You come into a distortionless state.

You can become more aware by meditating in this manner: "My form is the reflection of my own thoughts. There is no need to fight against it, complain about it, or waste time wishing that I had somebody else's form. Whatever I have I accept. I can use it for my growth. If it cannot attract people, it is all right. Now I am free to use this form for service. In this way, I will be able to get rid of all the forms. I am on the path to bringing an end to the cycle of birth and death. I am going to reach Enlightenment."

Often when you see some pleasant face or appealing form, your attention is driven in that direction. Whenever you are driven toward something in that way, the drive itself is the effect of hypnotism or unclear thinking. Anything which takes you out of your own Self in order to master, hold, or possess something or someone is an outside influence. That influence will subside only when you see in your experience that there is nothing in the world of forms which you can hold on to permanently.

Why does this kind of hypnotic trance occur? It occurs because of your having an obsession with the body. To break the dependency, you have to see the elements of the body as they are. Otherwise, there is no end to the ways in which mind and senses become entranced.

Now let us become more aware of the process the unaware mind goes through when it is influenced. Observe the person whose eye is attracted by a beautiful face; all the senses respond in that direction. He begins to have thoughts of how to meet, and before long his mind is making plans about the person. If he allows himself to be driven in this way, without checking his thought or behavior patterns, the circle of thinking will continue. By comparison with this new fantasy, his marriage and family will begin to seem dull and uninteresting. His mind will have gone somewhere else. So he uses all his energy to get what he expects to be fresh excitement. You can see that the cause of divorce is the mind in which the seed of attraction has taken root.

The mind continues to find some excuse to reinforce its growing seed of desire. The person who might otherwise have been bothered if his wife did not ask him, "What did you do today? Where were you?" now becomes irritated by these same questions. Before his mind started playing games with him, he would have appreciated her interest in his work. This same man now thinks, "My wife is putting her nose into my activities." Or he rationalizes by saying, "She is a hindrance to my growth. She doesn't give me space."

Once a person allows this seed of attraction to grow,

it becomes a weed. It gathers momentum and takes over the person's whole life. The person does not realize that this seed of attraction is none other than dependency, not seeing the body for what it is.

When you become aware of the way in which a hypnotic trance invades the unaware mind and covers it with body-consciousness, driving it to and fro in either attraction or aversion, you know the importance of seeing yourself as a flame within the candle. In order to break excessive concern with the body, the monks reflect on the lesson taught by the nineteenth prophet in Jain history, a woman named Mallinatha.

Malli was a beautiful princess, who lived in the land of Videha. From childhood everybody praised her flowering grace, her refined complexion, her serene manner. When she was eighteen years of age, poets were inspired to write verses about her and artists to paint her portrait. Everyone loved to talk about Princess Malli.

In their travels, merchants and ministers, goldsmiths and sculptors, brought news of her incomparable beauty to kings and princes from near and far. One called her the "most wonderful creation on earth," and another likened her to "fresh grapes on the vine." Still another compared her to "a shower of white roses," and a wandering nun who had seen her said she was like "the evening star." As soon as each of six kings of neighboring lands heard these words, he became impatient to marry the princess. Each sent a messenger with a letter to the king of Videha to request the hand of the princess in marriage.

The first to arrive delivered a letter which stated, "I am eager to marry your daughter, and for that I will do anything you require of me. However, if you do not accept my offer, it will breed war between my land and yours." The second messenger delivered a similar proposal. In a month, six such proposals came from the six infatuated kings of the neighboring lands. Hearing the same request from all six messengers, King Kumbhaka became alarmed and called upon his guards to drive them all away.

As a result, the six kings consulted one another and decided to join together to attack Videha. They came with their armies trailing behind them. While they awaited the king's answer, a large number of soldiers engulfed the small kingdom, placing the king in a trying position. He did not know what to do. He could not decide who should marry his daughter, and his army was not strong enough to force them to go home.

Malli noticed her father's distress and addressed him. "Father, dear, why are you worried? There is no need for concern. Send a message to each king that I am ready to marry."

"What?" he asked. "You are ready to marry? But which one? There are six!"

"Never mind," she answered calmly. "Invite each one separately to come to my palace alone after a fortnight's time and say that you are going to give me to him in marriage."

"To all six of them?" her father inquired incredulously.

"Yes!" she replied. "All six! Be sure not to tell one about the other. Let each one think he was invited alone!"

Seeing the flame of confidence in her eye and hearing the conviction in her voice, her father knew that the princess was fully aware of what she was doing. So he sent her message to each of the six kings separately.

A fortnight passed. On the appointed night, all six came to her door. When they saw one another, they could not understand why all six were there. They looked at each other and the coals of jealousy began to burn within each one's heart. Each had cherished the thought that the invitation was only to him. Each began to feel the pain which comes from striving to gain and fearing to lose a material thing—in this case, the hand of the princess in marriage.

Meanwhile, the princess came and opened the door. She invited them into her hall. To their surprise, they saw there a beautiful statue of Malli. Each feature was precisely the same as hers. It was life-size and made of gold. It was so bright that it dazzled their eyes. It was an exact replica of Malli and looked truly alive.

As the princess stood beside the statue, she greeted the kings, "Welcome to you! So, you have come here, have you? And do you want to marry me?" As they all murmured "Yes," Malli pressed a device behind the statue and a lid at the top opened up. All of a sudden there was such an offensive odor that the kings were completely confused and disturbed. They could not bear it.

"What is this?" they asked.

"Oh, it is nothing!" she explained in a matter-of-fact way. "When I heard you were all coming to seek my hand, I thought, 'How to receive them? They are coming here to marry whom, to marry what?' I wanted to know, 'Have they really come to marry me, or my body?' So at each meal, I would put a morsel of my food in the hollow part of this statue. It is a very small amount. I have been collecting a few morsels a day for only fifteen days, and yet it rots and gives off this odor."

The kings were both dazzled by the beauty and baffled by the smell. The pleasant and the nauseating—it was difficult for them to manage! In that confusion, they began to wonder why they had come.

Then the princess told them, "Let us go out of the room. Come and sit here with me. Why do you think that the six of you are attracted to me? Is it only beauty or is it something different? Now you know that beauty is only as deep as the skin. You have smelled the decomposing elements of the body and you did not like it. There is something more that has brought you here. It is that which attracts you, not the body. Close your eyes, meditate, and see."

In that moment of silence, a glimpse came to each of them. They saw that all seven of them had been together in a past life. They had been living a good life and all were spiritual aspirants. But there was still something binding them which they could not yet understand. It was some kind of leftover dependency. Because of that, they each had to take another birth. Otherwise, they would have reached Enlightenment in that very life.

As they caught that glimpse, they understood when Malli told them, "We are on the path to the Light, but in our last birth we forgot our glimpse of it; for a while we were blind. That is why we had to take this birth."

The kings told her, "Now we want you to guide us. You are our teacher. We want to finish this cycle of birth and death."

So she said to them, "The magnetism we feel is not toward the body but toward the soul. The soul remains together with this body while we journey through this human life. But the two are not to be confused. Each one has a completely different nature. So let us use this life to bring out the soul, to purify our awareness, to reach our destination of freedom."

The seven of them took the path to liberation together

and led a beautiful life. Malli ultimately became Mallinatha, the nineteenth Tirthankara, or "Perfect One." She is known in Jain history for having taught mankind how to differentiate between the pure flame of soul and the melting elements of the body.

We too must have that glimpse. We are here to move in that spiritual direction. If we remain obsessed only with the body, we will inevitably experience sorrow and heaviness. We will feel the pangs of separation. But if we experience that glimpse, then our intention will be to grow, to understand, to move toward the Higher Self. We will come to know one another on the level of soul. A union among friends which is an experience of inner divinity is not like other relationships. It is not subject to the pain of separation; it is becoming a permanent union.

If you want to read a book or a letter, you cannot put it right next to your eyes. You need some distance. You have to let the light fall on it. In the same way, when you know the nature of the flame and the wax, you give yourself some distance. You allow space between you and the ever-changing elements which constitute your body. You make room between you and the gravitating elements which cover your mind.

When you reach this state, you become the doctor of your body and mind. You become aware of your capacity to heal. Once you know the nature of the four elements—earth, water, fire, air—you pay attention to your body, as you do to any precious machine, to see which element is lacking. Then you locate the missing ingredient and bring yourself health.

Anyone who is clinging to the body is unable to do this kind of self-healing. It requires distance. Once you are no longer hypnotized by the body, you see it as it is. You stop spoiling it and experience oneness with your Self. In this way, you make contact with your deep wellspring of energy and restore your health.

Once you glimpse that sprouting, upward-moving element in you, you live with the world but not of it. Likewise, you live with the body but not of it. The body is the same; how you look at it makes the difference. This body is nothing to cling to; rather you use it to grow in awareness and to help others grow.

To see the body as an object of pleasure or gratification or as a means to relieve oneself from tension is really to misuse the body. To see it as a vehicle to bring communication and communion is to use it properly, with respect and care. Then it is truly a *premamandir,* a temple of love—a sacred place in which the flame of reverence extends to all living beings universally.

So be aware throughout your day to break the inner hypnotism. Know that no hold is strong enough to keep a worldly thing permanently. If your relationship is based on false perception, then it is a castle on the sand. When the sand shifts, it collapses. If you relate as soul to soul, as human being to human being, then your foundation is solid. Become aware day and night of how your awareness shifts from soul to form, from form to soul. Notice what happens in your feeling, in your consciousness when your perception changes.

Now glide into meditation and see in your heart a temple. Inside the temple is a shrine. In the heart of the shrine see a beautiful flame. See how the flame, your soul, is connected to a beautiful candle, your body. The flame and the candle join together. They meet to take you up. Together they become a torch for your progress and your growth.

Seed-Thoughts for Meditation

What is moving upward in me? It is my purity, my spirit's longing to find the beautiful, the noble, the divine.

What is melting downward in me? It is the dross, that which decomposes and disperses into its own elements.

Let me take the process of meditation to dehypnotize my consciousness. Do I know whether my actions come from self-awareness or from someone else's suggestion?

Nothing fetters or binds a person who is aware. He lives in the world, with the world, but not of it.

Let me live as a premamandir, *a temple of love, a sacred place in which I extend the flame of reverence to all living beings universally.*

FACET SEVEN

Observing the Inflow of Vibrations

THE aspirant who is treading the path to liberate himself must take care not to lose balance. Like a tight-rope walker, if he misses even one step, he could come plunging down to the ground and hurt himself. That is why he follows the practice of vigilance. He watches each step he takes. He becomes aware of each thought he receives and sends. He discovers the meaning of each relationship in which he engages.

For an aspirant, the danger which threatens his balance comes in the form of *ashrava,* meaning that which flows from all directions. There is a flow of vibrations which is constantly streaming into your consciousness from all sides. It is continually pushing and pulling, attracting and repelling, giving you ups and downs. From where does the flow come? From without and within, from society and from emotions, from your conditioning, from your mental structures, and from your background of repulsion and attraction. In this *bhavana,* the reflection is on *ashrava,* in order to become aware of the kind of inflow you are susceptible to, and to learn how to stop yourself from being swallowed up by it.

Many unpleasant thoughts and feelings have already entered your consciousness and are bothering you day and night. They don't allow you to be in a natural blissful mood. Balance is bliss. Our real state is to be in balance, in bliss. Unlike joy, which depends upon some prop or outside stimulus, bliss requires nothing. It is being with one's own Self. When you are in a state of balance, your consciousness can be seen for what it is, calm and clean and pure, like a clear mountain lake. Without balance, you are like a stormy sea, at times rolling in one direction, at other times rolling in another direction. You are either excited or depressed, in a state of constant fluctuation. In this unsteadiness, a lot of debris is collected in your consciousness, like pollutants entering a clear stream. The debris, or karma, which flows in and muddies your pristine consciousness has entered because of unawareness. You left all the outlets to your consciousness open, and now the debris has become mixed up with the pure waters.

In this reflection, there is one fundamental premise: the watcher is not the same as the inflow he is watching. You stand back from the process you are observing. You use *viveka,* the sense of discrimination. If a car does not work well, the driver does not compare himself with the car. If your house is old, you do not identify yourself with it. If your clothes are dirty, you do not consider yourself dirty. In the same way, when you notice dullness or heaviness or negativity, you do not identify with them. Those impurities are not you. They come from outside, and what has come from outside can go back outside. Such debris does not belong in your pure consciousness. On that premise you have to meditate.

In meditation, always see yourself as innocent, clean, and beautiful. Without condition, love yourself. Without guilt, see yourself. When you have love for yourself, you will be able to experience Self-Realization. Otherwise, if you allow the consciousness to become identified with the extraneous inflow, you may start blaming yourself.

You may put yourself down. You may focus on the dust which has collected around your soul instead of on the clean mirrorlike quality of your soul itself. And if you accept yourself as a sinner, you will live in that false nature. You will carry guilt wherever you go. Identifying yourself with that which binds you, how will you be able to free yourself from it?

So remember that sin and guilt do not belong to you. Keep before your mind's eye a beautiful image of yourself. Think of yourself as *arogya,* as a powerful dynamic energy, in complete spiritual health. In this way, mental uncertainty and confusion, which are the causes of most diseases, will disappear.

As you meditate, your belief in your innate purity will come not only from somebody's encouraging word, but from an inner glimpse. When you are alone, sitting by a calm lake, and nothing is bothering you, how do you feel? You watch the mellow evening slowly unfold its colors. How peaceful and blissful you feel! Your real nature reveals itself. Why? Because nothing is disturbing you.

That precious feeling may last five minutes, ten minutes, half an hour, but at least it can give you a glimpse. What lasts for a few minutes is able to last for an even longer time. It is a question of extension. So a brief glimpse gives you some conviction in your inherent peace. It gives you the courage to ask, "If such a glimpse was possible for a few moments, why not longer?" That kind of conviction is going to last long. It is not borrowed from anybody's assurance or promise; it comes from experiencing what is yours. According to your own experience, you move forward into deeper knowledge of your own Self.

* * *

So instead of going out, the aspirant goes in. What we call silence, detachment, or retreat is merely taking time to make the whole area of one's consciousness clean. It is a purification of the reservoir of our energy. There are three steps. First is a drying process. The waters of one's consciousness which have become dirty and polluted are temporarily allowed to dry up. The process of watching itself acts as a powerful heat energy to evaporate all negative vibrations. To take this step one has to make a decision to close off the gates, outlets, or passageways through which new pollutants could enter. Second, when one looks at the bedrock of one's consciousness, one pinpoints the mud or sticky residue in order to dig it out and remove it. Only when the area is completely clean does one throw open the gates and allow fresh water to flow in once again.

To embark on this process, sometimes people cut off relations with other people for a while. They need to give themselves some space. It is not running away from oneself or from the world. That interpretation of the word "detachment" is not appropriate. *Detachment is not going away from anybody; it is coming to your own Self.* To attach means to tie. To detach is to untie. Anything which binds you, which drags and pulls you, that is your tie. Because of this tie you are not in your own space. Something is pulling you from one end, and you do not feel steady.

Take some time to watch yourself. Remove yourself from complicated situations. Untie yourself from all the influences with the understanding that you want to see yourself clearly. The idea is not to escape from the world, but to prepare yourself to be with life, with your own life and with life at large. And how can you be with anyone if you are not first with your own Self? If you tell someone, "I will be with you" before you know yourself, you are giving a false promise. Instead, say to yourself,

"I want to be steady, not fickle. I want to stop this constant movement to and fro. Let me be with myself so that I will know how to be comfortable with others."

In this way, you see life as an inner laboratory. You put yourself on the test and ask yourself penetrating questions. "Am I comfortable with myself? Do I go to others to make them happy, or do I go in order to avoid myself?" If you are traveling here and there to escape yourself, then you are taking that uncomfortable feeling with you. Wherever you go, you are creating discomfort in those relationships. Try as you may to find a haven of safety away from yourself, you cannot escape your own restless feeling. The most difficult thing is this: to be comfortable with one's own Self in order to be comfortable with all.

Once a person kept to himself, meditating in silence. Three friends observed him and joked about him. "What is he doing?" they said, laughing. "He sits all day and does nothing. We can do that easily."

When the meditator heard this, he asked, "Do you think it is easy to be, just to be?"

"Yes," one friend answered, "you have nothing to do. I have so many responsibilities—to go to work, pay my rent, take care of my house. If you would take my place, I would gladly sit here like you."

"Very well," agreed the meditator. "I will take care of providing you with food. I will pay your rent and do everything that you usually do. It will be one month's program. What you have to do is to be with yourself."

The friend replied, "Oh, that will be easy. But what do I have to do in exchange?"

"Nothing," answered the meditator. "There is nothing to do, just to be. You will remain in this beautiful bungalow, and I will give you this word, *So-hum,* to recite."

"That's all? Only to recite the word?"

"Yes, that's all."

The agreement was made, and the friend was very happy. For the first two or three hours, he sat thinking, "Well, everything is taken care of. I don't need to worry about paying my rent."

And he started reciting the *mantra.* Four more hours passed. He got tired and a little bored sitting there. He started to think, "What am I doing? The same word over and over! Well, compared to the labor I was doing, it's not bad!" And he continued reciting the *mantra.*

The next day he went on. *"So-hum, So-hum,"* he repeated. "Such a dull sound! There is no song, no drum, no excitement! What is all this?"

He was sitting by the window with no one to talk to, with no one to listen to his jokes. He was taking all his meals by himself. By the third day, he began to feel heavy. On the fourth day, when he arose, he said to himself, "I will go crazy, I can't bear it!"

Thoughts from his subconscious had started coming, one after another. He thought of what kind of life he had lived, how he had played games with people, how he had cooked up so many lies. Each thing became magnified. In silence, that is what happens—things become magnified.

When you are suffering from too much heat, you can take off your clothes. But when there is suffocation of thoughts, how do you escape from them? It is so easy to change clothes, but how difficult it is to change thoughts! Thoughts carve so deep that they sometimes feel like thorns and give us pain.

This man was not ready to face himself. People have some device to cover up those things which they are not ready to face, to hide them or make them smaller. But on this day, for this person, things were becoming larger.

"No," he thought, "my mind will blow."

On the fifth day, he went back to his friend and told him, "I want out! I don't want to do this any more."

"What about our agreement?" his friend asked him.

"To hell with it!"

"Why are you using the word 'hell'?"

"Because I am suffering hell," he answered. "My thoughts have become monstrous."

"So," his friend gently chided him, "don't you think that one day you will have to face your own thoughts? Why not see them now? How long will you keep on running away from them? You are going to have to face them afterward, so why not start now? Why postpone?"

"Have I to face them?" asked the friend.

"The time comes to all; if not now, then later. One day, you will have to be alone. You will not be surrounded by people. Why not confront yourself now? You know how you feel after eating too much hot, spicy food. There is a burning sensation in your body. Your thoughts are percolating inside you like that, making you upset. You can't control them or get rid of them. Why not do something about them—change them?"

"What to do?" asked the new meditator. "How can I change my thoughts from what they are already?"

"Inside you are pure. You have to separate yourself from your thoughts, and watch them one by one. In the past, you left all your senses, the inner gates, open. You didn't know that when you use them to go out, at the same time they let dirty gutter water in. So now you need to dry up all the water. How can you see a good reflection of yourself when you are clouded by so much unclear thinking and entangled in superficial love affairs?"

"Then how can I live?"

The friend answered, "Live, yes, that is what you must do! But just now you are not really living. You are running away. Now is the time to be watchful and discriminating. Cleanse your consciousness and then you will feel your life."

When you meditate on the inflow of vibrations, you learn to detect which outlets are left open and what kind of debris is coming in. You watch the way in which you are vulnerable to negative habits. The antidote to *ashrava* is *samvara. Samvara* means to stop—to lock the gates and stop the inflow from continuing to flood in. The key to *samvara* is *ashrava.* You cannot effectively stop the inflow without first knowing of what it consists.

Ashrava bhavana teaches us how to observe our weaknesses, our unlocked gates, our inner ensnarements, our unchecked addictions. The first one is *kashaya,* which means inner passions or attachments, such as anger, pride, greed, and deceit. They are gangsters; all are in alliance with one another. They work in a clever way. They don't always appear all at once. One enters through the window first, unlocks the door, and lets in the others. They each have a subtle connection.

You may think, "I have only a little ego left." But if someone insults your ego, that brings anger. You may flare up and use harsh words. A person with ego has some deceit as well. In order to prevent his ego from receiving a puncture, he will do deceitful things. In that ego, there is also greed, to become more and more powerful, and to keep others in a subordinate position. Moreover, if someone gets in the way of the greedy person when he is collecting something, whether it is a material thing or a high post, he will be angry. So these four, known as *kashaya,* open the door to the gutter rather than to the fresh rainfall. This is the first gate which must be closed.

Secondly, there is an open gate or ensnarement called *yoga.* It has a special meaning in this context. It is the *yoga* by which mind, word, and body are connected or glued to tempting, alluring, enticing things. Such things constantly pull you when you are unaware. For example, if you go window-shopping and see a coat, your eye connects with the coat and your mind becomes filled with plans of how to get the money to buy it. If the person you live with does not help you out financially, you become angry. "What do you do for me?" you complain. "You won't even help me buy a beautiful coat."

All your energy is pulled in the direction of collecting enough money to buy the coat. This demonstrates the way in which the senses connect with attractive things when the gate of *yoga* is left open, unchecked by awareness.

A third ensnarement is called *pramada,* or lethargy. It comes in three forms to muddy the waters of our consciousness. First, there is indecisiveness. The person is wishy-washy and goes in all directions. Such a person is unaware of himself; that is why he can be pushed or pulled in conflicting ways. There is no purposeful direction to his life; rather, he moves in a rut or a vicious circle.

Related to this is a second form of *pramada:* non-attention to time or lack of discipline. People who tend to be lazy say, "I don't have time," because they don't know how to use time. Such a person knows how to waste time. He may go on sipping coffee for hours, or watching television or reading the papers, until it becomes late and he must rush off to his appointment. That shows no arrangement of time. It's an ensnarement which saps one's energy. But one who knows how to harness time always has time.

The third form of *pramada* is not being aware of life,

not caring for one's own Self. There are people who have not taught themselves to know how to use this beautiful gift of human life. It requires some discipline and some commitment. That is why people who practice *apramada,* or awareness, outline their program. It is not too rigid. But they know what they want to accomplish in a day, in a month, in a year, so that they can use their energy in that direction. It is not accomplishing for the sake of achievement or outer reward; it is engaging oneself in some purposeful endeavor for the sake of life's growth and for the service of living beings. By keeping this awareness in the back of the mind, and attuning oneself to life, one can concentrate on the immediate work of the present moment and bring past, present, and future in harmony with one another.

If you have decisiveness along with some discipline, everything goes smoothly. You find the right balance in the allotment of time, taking a certain amount for peace, for meditation, for rest, for nutrition, for physical activity, and for service.

The fourth gate is an inner trap called *avirati,* failure to limit the things one needs and uses in life. To offset this neglect, the aspirant observes *virati,* a vow to place a limit on his possessions, his needs. It may be a vow to limit his food. He may say, "Today I am going to take only three kinds of food," or "Today I am going to eat only two meals," or "Today I will eat only unsalted, tasteless food."

In this way, the digestive machine does not get overloaded. Our system needs at least three hours in which to digest anything. If we throw in more food in less than three hours, it stops the system from continuing to digest the food which is already there. It has to go back and start all over again. If we limit our food intake, the system works accurately and indigestion does not occur. At the same time, to keep the body cool and to avoid constipation, liquids are taken eight or ten times a day. This method of systematic and balanced eating is a way to control one's taste buds, limit one's need, and preserve one's health.

There is no need to follow anything blindly. There is no compulsion to copy a monk's life. It must be done according to your environment. You must adjust and modify, rather than follow a system which was right for a certain climate, atmosphere, or period of time. What counts is the longing to limit your need. For example, you can make a commitment to limit your wealth. You make an agreement with yourself, "I am going to be satisfied with just this much." Otherwise, the mind will justify all that it wants, not what it needs. There is no need to earn right up until the last day. When one puts a limit, saying, "This is enough," then the time can be spent for spiritual unfoldment and service.

The fifth ensnarement is *mithyathva*—ignorance and confusion. In *mithyathva,* truth is mixed up with lie, violence is confused with non-violence, lust is taken for love, and right is undifferentiated from wrong. It reflects muddled thinking. It shows the inability to discriminate between what is compassionate and what is hurtful. For example, a person whose mind is darkened with *mithyathva* may be preaching universal love and at the same time approving the sacrifice of animals.

Mithyathva indicates failure to see the truth. Semi-truth is taken as truth and sometimes becomes more compelling than truth itself. It may bind, tie, and obsess you. Truth, on the other hand, is all light; it frees you. *Mithyathva* is the most serious ensnarement because of the way it takes hold inside.

These are the five gateways which allow the *shrava* to flow from outside to inside. When they are left open, our pure consciousness is vulnerable to innumerable pollutants, inner weaknesses, and deceptions.

Everything from the past and present has made an imprint on your consciousness—culture, family, geographical conditions, schooling, religious background. Some of the imprints we call worldly *shrava.* Others we call religious *shrava.* Though we may try to avoid worldly influences, sometimes religious imprints are even more of a burden. That is because they lead to an indelible kind of inner *shrava*—guilt, self-hatred, faultfinding, blind faith.

We have to see both, flow from without and flow from within. Inner dogma is that which prevents you from accepting yourself as you are. When someone criticizes you, you feel as if an arrow were piercing your heart. You feel psychological pain. You experience fear, and fear prevents you from living life.

The inner habit of self-criticism does not allow you to clear your consciousness of its load, of its muddy residue. Don't be overcritical of yourself, or you won't have the energy to work and go further. To be spiritual, you need lightness. No person became enlightened carrying the load of sadness. It is a heavy lump of clay. Being sad, you cannot see yourself. All the so-called sins (I call them consequences) are born from sadness. When someone is sad, he has identified so completely with that heaviness that he does whatever he can to escape. So he escapes into alcohol, drugs, or other vices. He may even commit suicide.

Enlightenment comes in a state of lightness. Guard against anything which makes you bleak, depressed, and cheerless. Do not allow it to arise, for once it comes, it clouds your whole vision. Without clear visibility, how can you see that you are in essence clean and pure?

Your consciousness needs clear open space. That is its nature—to be limitless, infinite, luminous. Meditating on *ashrava,* see how things have taken over your inner space. This may be reflected in your outer place. I have seen some homes where the furniture crowds the people. Do you often bump into your furniture? Now see whether or not in your consciousness you bump into objects, possessions, worries.

Go further and ask yourself, "Why do I buy things? Is it because I have left open the gate of *yoga?* Do I allow my eyes to be attracted to something and do I then run out and buy it? Is it because of ego? Do I buy things for my own use or for showing other people? Why am I trying to impress people? Why should I make my house into a furniture store?" See the obsession—when you have something, you want to show it, and when you don't have something, you feel mistreated for not having received it. Both are complexes; both stem from ignorance of Self.

Life itself is free from complexes, free from push and pull. There are so many commercials bombarding you. It is difficult to live in the world; it is easy to live in the forest. So you aspirants who live in the city have to be more careful than those who retired to the forest. For them there was no outer temptation. But for you there is constant temptation and you are learning to balance it.

Perhaps people make fun of you for being vegetarian. They call you crazy and shoot arrows of criticism at you. They may taunt you for wanting to live a natural life, for not wanting to be promiscuous, for not drinking wine, or for not going to an analyst. For them the abnormal is made normal. They do not realize that by going to sex seminars, for example, they are creating more desires, inner turmoil, pain, complexes, and breakups in their relationships rather than fewer. But you are sincere seekers. Throughout all the criticisms, you remain yourselves. You have the courage of inner conviction.

You have taken the time to experience the depth of life. You are not influenced by ephemeral things. You have meditated to find something lasting, something permanent, something which can give you inner confidence. When a strong gust of wind comes, you know how to stand and wait. It is the art of knowing how to withstand the tide before it engulfs you.

Once you have closed the open gates, dried up all the polluted water, and cleaned out all the debris, then you can open them again to receive the fresh, clean rainfall. What is that rainfall? It is the flow of *maitri*—pure love, compassion, and communication. You feel free and flowing with all. You are not meeting people to impress them. You meet to share. See how easily you meet people when there is no feeling of greater or lesser, no scar or bitterness, no faultfinding or criticism.

And when somebody criticizes you, you will be able to accept it as an indication that perhaps there is something in you which you have not yet uprooted. So you will be grateful to that person for pointing out to you yet another way in which to grow and lighten your burden. If you are sincere in your approach to living, then even one who used to find fault with you or dislike you will find room in his heart for you.

Enlightened people do not close themselves off in their own world. Knowing what they are in essence, they talk and move in the world without being polluted by anything. They learn to act without *kashaya,* so that no more dust and debris will be invited to cling to their pure consciousness and cover their visibility. If you put your whole heart into working on this seriously, you can change your life style. Instead of making the world a valley of unhappiness, you can transform it into a garden of bliss.

You can live in total freedom—in yourself, in your own space, not in somebody else's space. Free from being driven by the inflow of negative vibrations, you are free to dwell in your own natural state, to flow in your own pure stream of blissful consciousness.

Seed-Thoughts for Meditation

Let me see my consciousness as a clean body of water, clear, pure, and sparkling.

When I stand back, I can watch the inflow of negative vibrations. I have no need to identify with them, for what has come from outside can go back outside. It does not belong in my consciousness.

My real nature is blissfulness. When I am in this natural state, I am in balance.

Detachment is not going away from anybody; it is coming to my own Self. Let me be with myself; then I will know how to be with you.

Faith that comes from somebody else's word, promise, or prediction is not going to last long, because it is borrowed. Conviction which comes from inner experience is going to endure.

Instead of making the world a valley of unhappiness, I can transform it into a garden of bliss with awareness.

FACET EIGHT

The Art of the Full Stop

AS seekers, you are like mountain climbers. Your climb is to reach the height of your consciousness. Whether it is a mountain or your own Self, to reach the peak you must climb in stages, one step at a time. The higher you go, the more careful you have to be. The wind at the top is very strong. If you are not well balanced, it can throw you back. When we observe the lives of great people, we are moved by their achievements, but we may not consider how much awareness and balance it took for them to reach that height. On all sides, there were always temptations and alluring things to divert the attention. At times there was fear of falling into the valley below. Despite all the potential deterrents, they went on steadily, because their whole intention was to reach the top.

They always kept their purpose in front of their inner eye. They had to be vigilant, careful, aware, and balanced. Why did they want to reach the peak? Because from there one can experience the freshest air, the panoramic view, the joy of seeing the beauty of the earth below and the skies above.

No one on the ground can imagine what the person who climbs Mount Everest has to go through. It is constant vigilance. Only when you start climbing do you realize how steep the path is, how high the peak. But if you have inside courage, conviction, and confidence, then you are not afraid. "I am going to make it," you say to yourself.

And you *are* going to make it, because there is no agent outside of you determining your life, making it prosperous or not. As a seeker, you accept the responsibility for each act. You realize, "If I am responsible for my own steps, then there is no danger. I am going to reach my destination because I am here for that."

You may accept somebody's helping hand as you move along the path, but that help is second to your own. Yours is first. In this way, you are neither arrogant nor falsely modest; both attitudes are extreme. Both mean pretension. A person who is trying to cut a figure in society or make a name for himself may play the role of being as submissive as a lapdog in order to draw some kind of attention. It is a trick. When you are aware of being humble, you want people to notice how simple you are. Why do you want to tell everybody? It means you need to capitalize on that.

Be natural, be what you are! Only watch *where* you are! Watching, you will become so subtle that you will know where you are at all times. If you can know that, it is enough. Then you won't need to ask approval from the world. When you finally don't need approval, that is when the world is ready to give it to you. It appears a little paradoxical. But people start sensing your genuineness. "Really this person is not on a trip," they observe. "She is with herself."

The fact is we are here just to live, just to be, not to collect trophies, degrees, and certificates. Our whole approach is to be what we are. We are not here for some temporary height, for some false inflated sense of who we are. Our aim is to return to that natural state which is so balanced that we are neither down nor up. For that we have to work in a wholehearted way. We can move toward that natural state only if we refrain from despising, criticizing, and abusing ourselves. We stop the craving to collect opinions, words of praise, and approval. When we put a stop to the inflow of such old habits of thinking, how peacefully we start living!

There is no greater joy in the world than to have peace with oneself. That is the real reason behind our seeking all kinds of joy. We want to remain in a beautiful mood. But when we see that temporary joy depends on outside stimulation and often brings sadness when its time is over, then we realize that it is essential to learn how to be at home with ourselves and discover permanent peace.

It does not mean that you reject the outside world. You appreciate the beauty and bounty of the world. You have five beautiful senses. In fact, your senses are kept so clear and clean that you can appreciate more keenly than most people the many sights and sounds, tastes and smells, feelings and perceptions. When something beautiful appears before you, you see it as it is. The point is this: you are not dependent solely on your senses. When you close your eyes, there also is beauty. So you see both the beauty within and the beauty without.

The problem with most of us is that we see the beauty without but not the loveliness within. Isn't it strange that after so many years of seeing beauty without, still we are unable to retain it when we close our eyes? As soon as we close our eyes, we see darkness. What is the point of all those years of enjoying outer beauty if they have not given us a clue to our inner beauty? It is wonderful to open the eyes and appreciate the beauty of sunrise, springtime, children dancing, and mellow faces whose wrinkles tell the story of joy and pain. *But there is richness within, our moving spirit.*

Without that moving spirit, the outer eyes would not perceive even the outer world.

We have to know that moving spirit whose capacity it is to experience, remember, and grow. Because of its presence, we are longing to quench our inner thirst. It is our true identity. It is sitting inside our outer shell. Meditating on this, we realize, "What I have been calling 'me' is only the shell. It is my instrument. The essence is inside. That essence is me."

The initiate watches inside and climbs each step of awareness until he reaches the core, the inner shrine. Ultimately, you reach that shrine and sit on the throne which is waiting for you. People call it God's throne. It is not reserved for only a few. It is waiting for all. Each of us has that throne within. That is why we have a longing, a dream, a quest. That archetype, that throne sometimes beckons to us, "Come unto me!" So the initiate moves.

But in order to move and ascend to the peak you have to be free from the load. If you have too much of a burden, you cannot carry it along with you. Gravitational forces are there to pull you down. The Buddha was not a foolish person to leave the palace and his beautiful wife and child. He was not a dropout. He had a quest for truth. And Mahavir was not a silly person when he talked to his wife, saying, "Where is our kingdom, dear? Is it only on earth? This kind of kingdom will perish. This kind of kingdom creates fights and wars. Can we not have that kingdom which is eternal awareness?" In this way, giving up becomes a receiving. *True renunciation is full awareness of the kingdom within.*

That inner level will also bring deep meaning to relationships. When husband and wife inspire each other, they become beautiful company for one another. Their communication turns into an eternal communion. The idea in marriage is to work out karmas and be a complement to each other. When we live on that inner level, we communicate and find out what is our mission. And when one feels low, the other is a lifting spirit. "This will pass," he tells his partner. "We have to be patient and wait for the sunrise." When one person is moody, there is no need for the other to add to the misery. There is no permanent pain nor is there any permanent bubbling happiness. What is permanent? Inner bliss, tranquillity; all else comes and goes.

To see the nature of the outer world and to experience the beauty of the inner world there is no need to go to a monastery. You can turn your house into a monastery! After all, some monasteries themselves have turned into political arenas for people to express their power drive!

I wish each family, each of you, could turn your small house into a beautiful monastery and create a beautiful life there, growing in understanding and meaning. Seventy or eighty years, our time on earth, is such a short period. You can use it to be alone or to be with people who share your thinking and understanding. You can use it to be with friends or neighbors or to be with whomever you feel love and compassion for. The world does not belong to anyone. There is no need for pettiness or limitation. There is no restriction of caste, creed, age, color, or language. We can all speak the same language —of eye and heart and feeling.

Samvara means to stop the flow of *ashrava.* First we meditated on *ashrava,* to know what the flow consists of, and where it is coming from—without and within. Once we know how it works, we stop it.

When a rainstorm is coming, and you hear on the radio that it is going to be a severe one, what do you do? Do you not become careful and take precautions? Don't you get up and close the windows, gather up any equipment lying outside on the lawn, bring it in, and stay inside? If you don't close the windows, what will happen? The house will be filled with dust and dirt and rainwater.

Samvara means to close the windows when the storm is about to come. In life the storm is *kashaya*—anger, greed, pride, and deceit. Anger is a storm. When it comes, first it upsets our own peace. Then it destroys what is around it. Anger distorts, blinds, and prevents clear vision. The person whose heart and eyes are burning with anger does not like anything beautiful. Smile at the person, and you will see that your smile is not tolerated. "Why are you smiling?" he will roar at you.

When you are angry, your child may come rushing over to you. "Mummy!" he cries, but you say, "Go away," and you push him aside. Your friend comes and you destroy ten years of friendship in ten minutes. "I hate you"—those words can create a big impact on the consciousness. How to erase them? You can say, "I am sorry," but that does not take away the sting of the words. They pierce like an arrow, and someone's heart is bleeding. The pain and the wound remain. Why do you use such harsh words? I do not say that you should suppress anger, but watch from where it has come. Feel the words you are throwing out. They are going to have repercussions, both in you and in someone else. Every word has a vibration which has an impact on your consciousness.

Once a woodcutter went into the forest and saw a lion. He became frightened. The lion took pity on him and told him where to find some ornaments which were buried in the forest. The woodcutter was very happy, because he needed the money which the ornaments would bring for his daughter's marriage feast. He invited the guests, and along with them, out of gratitude to the lion, he invited the lion. The lion was not anxious to go to the party, but the woodcutter convinced him.

When he arrived, all the guests were alarmed and started to run away. "Don't worry," the woodcutter told them. "He won't hurt you. This lion is just as tame as an old dog."

When the money from the ornaments ran out, the woodcutter again went to the forest. This time the lion would not show him where there were more ornaments. Instead, he told him, "Here, make a wound on my paw with your knife."

The woodcutter asked, "What? You want me to make a cut in your paw?"

"Yes," the lion answered. "Come back in one month and I will talk to you then." He did as the lion requested, and one month later returned to the forest.

The lion asked him, "Can you see the wound you made with your knife?" The woodcutter saw that it was completely healed. The lion continued, "The wound of the flesh can be healed, but the wound from your words is still bleeding." The woodcutter had used the words "He is just as tame as an old dog" in a hurry, and the lion was insulted at being compared to a dog.

So when anger is about to come and you are about to speak harsh words, say to yourself, "Let me close the window." The first window to close is the mouth. It is better to close the mouth and open the eyes and see who is standing before you. There is no need to repress the anger. Watch the inside feeling and turn it into steam, into some creative energy. Let there be space between you and the person with whom you are angry. First you say to yourself, "I am angry. I don't like what happened."

At the same time, you use *samvara,* you stop yourself from speaking out. If you speak from a level of imbalance, when the anger is giving too much energy, your words will be amplified. So tell yourself to wait for your normal state to return.

Then ponder, "What is the cause of this anger? Did someone else make the mistake or did I have a part in it? Are not two hands needed to make a clap? Can it be avoided in the future? What are the ways to prevent it?" When you have this spirit of inquiry, this space, you don't allow the energy of anger to go out. You keep it in for the time being like a pressure cooker. You let the steam out very slowly.

After that, instead of using a lot of words, you select a few words and tell the person very gently, "This is what made me angry. I would prefer this," or "This has spoiled my peace. I don't want to spoil your peace with my anger." In this way, you stop the cycle of action, reaction, and interaction. You see the pain that anger has caused and you do not want to evoke it in someone else. You want it to end here. With a gentle feeling toward the other person, you can awaken his or her consciousness. By shouting, what are you going to accomplish?

So follow these three steps when anger comes. First, be aware of your feeling. What was your expectation which created the sensations in your body, the increasing buildup of hot energy. Second, retain the energy until your balance returns. Do not allow yourself to speak. Third, when you are feeling calm, tell the person what has made you unhappy, what has hurt your feelings. Your very gentle selective words will start working on that person's consciousness if the person is sensitive. If the person cannot understand you, even your shouting will have no meaning.

Another storm is the storm of pride. When pride inflates you like a balloon and you say, "I want to be greater than that person," notice its cruel aspect. The ego makes you want to surpass and make the other person feel inferior to you. If you were not cruel, you would not do anything to make another feel beneath you. This inner cruelty comes from complete unawareness of Self.

On the contrary, we must try to make a person feel at home. Know that the things you have are for sharing, for peace, for comfort, for communication; they are not for impressing others or for creating a difference in levels. Find out how you really feel about things. Things themselves are unimportant; it is your attitude which counts. Ask yourself, "Am I playing a game? Am I really with people or am I trying to be superior?" To be with people is excellent; to act superior is a result of ignorance.

Pride or ego is not the same as self-respect. Ego has a way of invading the whole cerebral area and causing a vicious circle of behavior. Self-respect radiates from inner awareness, from inner balance. Ego depends on the external situation; self-respect is steady on all occasions. Ego acts like mercury in a thermometer, going up and down according to the heat. Self-respect has its own poise, the outer climate does not affect it. The aspirant is one who keeps balance.

The third inner enemy is greed. Once greed takes hold of us, our needs continue to expand. We keep on changing our standards. Greed tears people into pieces, and the inside pain that results cannot be cured with any medicine. Many people who have reached the top of the political, business, or religious hierarchy have torn themselves apart with misery when forced to retire and pass their days in a small way. They had lived from pomp, but when their situations changed like the weather and their ego desires were no longer satisfied, they felt utter frustration. For them, it was a mental torture.

Only if such people have a hobby can they survive.

Eliminating greed does not mean you should not earn a living. It involves asking yourself this question: "Am I comparing myself with someone else or am I happy with what I have?" Greed is like a powerful earthquake. It can cause havoc in one's life. So you practice the art of the full stop and say, "Enough!"

When you have anger, ego, and greed, then the fourth inner enemy comes—deceit. To maintain the first three, you have to play a role. You have to pretend to be what you are not. You always have to be on your toes. You are not natural. You are always putting on a mask or covering yourself with makeup. It is not easy to keep up the façade. One day you will get up from your slumber and find yourself without any makeup. It is far better to reflect on how to stop and see yourself, how to be what you are.

As you practice *samvara,* you understand its purpose. It is for your *arogya*—your spiritual health. If your longing to climb to the height of yourself is genuine, you will want inner health. It will not be to please or show anybody else; it will be for yourself. Just as you brush your teeth to keep them clean and fresh for your own feeling of well-being, so you cleanse your consciousness of impure elements. Just as you wash your body to feel refreshed and not to show how soft your skin is, in the same way you unclog the pores of your mind in order to think clearly, without distortion. The highest soul uses meditation to keep *arogya.* Practicing in this way, he or she has no need for any temporary lift from the outer world. The aspirant does not want anything temporary; he or she wants only that insight which is going to last forever.

So when the storm of anger, ego, greed, or deceit is

about to invade your consciousness, keep the word *samvara* in front of you. Tell yourself, "No, let me stop. Let me keep quiet. Let me not react. Let me not be cruel." Keeping a space between you and negative vibrations, you are able to deflect the vibrations. They will evaporate into thin air under the light of your ever-present awareness. In this way, you are able to stop the continuous inflow of karmas into the waters of your consciousness. You will be able to see clearly into your depths and remove the residue.

Seed-Thoughts for Meditation

Close the windows when the storm is about to come. In life the storm is anger, greed, ego, and deceit.

Let me see the pain anger has caused me so that I will not want to evoke it in anyone else.

Let me see the inner cruelty of greed, how in taking more than my share, someone else has to have less.

Let me see how the ego wants to put someone else down.

Let me see the pretension in deceit, how it is centered on covering up the truth from myself and the world.

If I keep the purpose always in front of my inner eye, I will make it to the peak. I am going to make it because there is no outside agent determining my life. I am here for that purpose.

FACET NINE

The Art of Cleansing

OBSERVE the way in which a river goes to the ocean. Why does it reach the ocean? Because it has two banks preventing it from becoming scattered. The banks protect and guide it, giving it the freedom to move and reach its destination. Without this protection, it does not find the ocean. If, instead, the river fights and breaks the two banks, it will dry up and die in the desert.

In a way, life is like a flowing river. We have the quest for truth, for reality. To find our ocean, our treasure, we have to be consistent and dedicated. If our mind is scattered, our energy will be dissipated, and we will never reach the ocean, our reality. But if we keep two banks on either side of us, we will keep our freedom to move, our energy to flow, and ultimately we will reach our Self.

What are the banks which we can build to guide us toward our reality? They are known as disciplines. These disciplines are not outside commandments laying down the laws of "Thou shalt" or "Thou shalt not." There is a difference between laws, or vows, and what we call disciplines. Vows are imposed from outside compulsion, whereas disciplines flow from inner self-awareness. They come from realizing that to do otherwise would be to become lost. They arise from the understanding that to dissipate one's energy is to abandon oneself to the wasteland. By listening to inner awareness instead of to outside compulsion, you know what you want and what you don't want.

When you prepare yourself through self-awareness, you take responsibility for each act you do, for each sentence you utter, for each thought you think. You are no longer random. You scrutinize. You know what you are taking in and what you are keeping out. You realize that once something unwanted enters your consciousness, it takes root. So you say to yourself, "Why do I take it?"

Scrutiny of thought, of speech, of relationships becomes second nature to you. You are aware of the law —that anything which comes into contact with you creates ripples or waves in your life. Ultimately, they disturb your peace, your calmness. So you take a little time to reflect on your whole life and your real needs. Herein rests the responsibility—to ask yourself, "What do I want? Why do I want? How much do I want?"

Everything is there, but we must learn how to select. As we go on asking those questions, slowly we understand that the world is like a candy store and that sometimes we are like children. Candies are colorful. They are beautifully wrapped. They attract us, and before we know it, we swallow them, not knowing how they will affect our health, our teeth, or our blood-sugar level. When our mind is in a childish, immature state, it likes to grab whatever it is given. At the same time, it has the tendency to want more and more. Once grabbing enters one's life, it works like sugar entering the bloodstream. There is an instant energy, a temporary "high," but afterwards the person's energy deflates with double speed.

That is why inner disciplines are inevitably necessary.

Without them, we will be ruled by a mind constantly floating and fluctuating between a high tide of joy and a low tide of depression.

The seers in their search found these twelve reflections in which they could sit, meditate, and see with balanced vision. The seventh, eighth, and ninth facets—*ashrava, samvara,* and *nirjara*—are deeply connected with one another. In *ashrava,* there is observation of the influx, of the open gates, of inner vulnerable points. In *samvara,* there is an action—of stopping the unwanted elements from coming in. It is closing the gates of the lake of consciousness. *Nirjara* is cleansing out the negative vibrations which have already accumulated and taken dominance in your consciousness.

You are in an observation tower. What do you find when you scan your life from this distance? You find your addictions. They may be smoking, drinking, overeating, overindulgence in sex, greed for wealth or fame. They all create weakness. All are props to support the crumbling house. No one is going to become stronger by depending on an addiction.

So the aware person asks, "When did this addiction start? How weak have I become? I am not at peace. I am not with myself. Because of this addiction, I am creating scars in my life. I go in search of happiness and end up finding pain." The seeker continues to go deep into his self-inquiry. "In pursuit of so-called enjoyment, my mind drives me in many directions. In the end, when I sit and watch, what do I get? In so many years, is there any happiness which gives me exhilaration, which lifts me? Or do I look upon past moments with sadness? Do my memories hover over me like a black cloud?"

By observing in this way, you come to the origin of your thoughts, the source of your needs; you see the quality of your desires and the meaning behind your relationships. When you see what kinds of thoughts come to you, you see why they come. What is their connection with you? Thoughts don't come unless there is a connection. If you haven't seen or heard something in relation to those kinds of thoughts, they won't occur in the mind. They arise because of the connection.

The next step comes: you see unwanted thoughts as invaders. You are sure that you don't want them, so you ask yourself, "Why do I allow them? Can I not exert my energy to stop them? Can I not bring out my willpower, my *Atma-virya?* Do I not have this soul power?" You become aware of your power. You exert your will, saying, "What I don't want must not come in."

When you take time to stop the intrusion of unwanted elements, your practice is born from inner awareness of your own power and of the direction you want to take in life. What you do is the result of a natural flow, not outside compulsion.

In *samvara,* you are with yourself. If new commitments or new relationships are continually coming, you are not able to see your thoughts, your emotions, your life. When you stop, you are in a position to watch. Then you ascertain which are the thoughts you do not want. "Let them not come," you assert. If the thoughts continue to bombard you, you realize you have some weakness inside. Because of the weakness, although you don't want those thoughts, you allow them to come. Stopping to observe yourself, you discover the addictions which are binding or conditioning you.

Bandha means to bind. When you look at your addictions from the point of view of the law of karma, you see that those inner weaknesses are binding you to matter. When you are in a state of either infatuation or hatred, you are not in your own nature. Your energy flow is blocked. Your soul is not free to move toward its destination. Some residue of matter remains like a cloud over your soul and influences your consciousness. Because of this influence, you think, speak, or act in an unaware or distorted way—with *kashaya,* passion. In this way, the residue acts like a gravitational force drawing to you particles of matter of a similar quality. If you hold on to this residue, though you try to take off, the overload will drag you down.

This ninth step is the antidote to *bandha,* or bondage. It is called *nirjara. Nirjara* means dropping, breaking off, and shedding away the binding elements, the addictions and attachments.

First let us see the mechanism of dropping this sticky residue. We think things are holding us, but in reality, we are the ones holding on to them. There was a monkey who put his hand into a small earthen pot and got a handful of chickpeas. But the mouth of the pot was very narrow, and when the monkey tried to pull his hand out, he could not. So he started shouting, "This pot is holding my hand!" Then a monkey trainer came and gave the monkey a spanking. "Silly monkey! Your hand is caught in the pot because you are holding on to so many chickpeas!" He dropped the chickpeas, and his hand was free.

The same thing happens in our life. We are greedy and we hold on to things. Drop that addiction which is binding you and you are free! No one is bound in the world. What binds you is your own addiction.

Unfortunately, one form of addiction is unhappiness itself. For example, what happens when people don't support your addiction? You think they are not being friendly toward you. Or watch what happens when you come home from work. By the end of the day, what have you collected from your communications with people? Either you take other people's emotional problems onto your own head or you blame others for your problems. Do you sit and chew on them at night? If so, it shows that you invite problems, that you are in some way addicted to unhappiness.

The sincere seeker goes deep. In order to drop the negative vibrations or addictions, he or she asks, "Are people really making me unhappy? Or am I taking their vibrations upon me because of my own addiction? If I am responsible, let me stop allowing this to happen. I want to drop all addictions."

Now a new understanding dawns upon you. When you reach this state, anyone who upsets you becomes your teacher. Anyone who causes you sorrow, pain, anger, jealousy, or ego becomes your guru. Why? Because he or she makes you aware of an addiction which was lying dormant in you. The hidden weakness is brought out in the open. So you say, "Thank you. It is good that you have made me aware of my preset response. Otherwise, I would not have known about it."

What do you do when a doctor tells you there is a cyst in your body? Do you say, "What a nasty person you are, telling me about it"? On the contrary, you say, "Thank you for making me aware of it. Please examine it." You have it checked and you pay the doctor for this service. In this way, the doctor makes you aware of your physical problem before it increases. You don't despise yourself because you have a cyst or a toothache or a virus. You say, "I have taken in something wrong or I have exposed myself to something unhealthy. That is why this disease has occurred. Let me check it now before it develops further."

In the same way, you don't hate yourself because you have an addiction. When you find it, you should not criticize yourself. If you put yourself down because of it, you become one with it. When you become one with your addiction, how can you separate from it? Thinking of yourself as hopeless and helpless, how can you move away from the weakness? You can separate yourself only if you have not become one with it.

So you see yourself as *Param-Atman,* as pure Self, perfect through and through. After all, your aim ultimately is to realize what you are. There must be clarity of vision. If the soul were by nature unworthy, how could you ever free yourself? If the soul were sinful from the beginning, how could it ever appear sparkling and clean? *To be pure and guiltless is your birthright.*

Certain addictions become like heavy colors. They color your inner vision so that you doubt your own Self. You lose sight of the fact that you are pure at heart, divine by nature. Just as you take some strong detergent to remove the heavy soil from your clothes, so you take the powerful light of meditation to rub out the influence which makes you see yourself as anything less than divine.

Your real Self is the steady, clear background. See your addictions as an influence, as a virus. Work on that level. Though they do not go easily because of being rooted in the long-distant past, still if you are serious about dropping them, they cannot remain.

There are certain trees which never grow high though they live a long time. That is because their roots are pruned and cut.

For any living thing to grow, its roots have to have room. Observe what happens when you put something in a particular condition. The condition limits the growth. Anything we have done for a long time and which we continue to do becomes a condition. It becomes cemented as part of our thinking. It makes itself so much at home in our consciousness that we are not ready to break with it. Even when we think that the condition is not going to last, we allow the mind to fool us and trick us into holding on to the condition in subtle ways. We forget the pain it can cause us. In this way, we become like those bonsai trees, dwarfed by our conditioning. If we never break it, we cannot grow and stretch. Without growing and stretching, we cannot reach our true height.

The idea in this second step is to break the conditions and free yourself. You want to free yourself so you can grow. You don't want to remain in a dwarfish mentality. If you do, you will deprive yourself of the infinite sky. So you make the decision to detect which conditions are limiting you and to break them. Then you will soar to the height and have the ecstasy of knowing your own Self.

The third step comes naturally. It is a shedding process. You are shedding the dry leaves from your life, because you are preparing for freshness. What happens when you do this? You discover the difference between "I" and "we." This "we" is the "we" of the herd mentality. When you live with "we," you always try to be like others. You feel inadequate and think, "What will people think of me if I speak? What if they laugh at me?" If you are not able to fit into what others are doing, you feel awkward and call yourself a "misfit."

Shed this misreading of yourself. Realize your uniqueness and tell yourself, "I am I. I can't be anything else. Whether others accept or reject me makes no difference. I am what I am." When you become what you are, a natural flow comes in your life. You begin to communicate with all without fear or inhibition. This is what I call separating out "I" from "we."

When "I" is mixed up with "we," it is drowned in a big ocean. How will you find your true "I" unless you stop comparing yourself with others? There are so many styles, languages, customs. Will you try to copy "we" all over the world? You may be able to succeed in one place, but there are so many other places. Where will it stop? Where will there be the variety of human life?

It is better to feel, "Wherever I go, I go with myself. I go with my uniqueness. Everywhere I will add my light, my fresh color, my new approach." It is a process of accepting your "I." This "I" has come alone and this "I" goes alone; ultimately, you love to be with yourself. At the same time, you communicate with all.

When you drop the outer coverings, you become creative. During the process, if you break down one shell and find still another one underneath, then you know that something is still left over. The time comes when you find nothing more to break. That is you.

When you find yourself, you realize, "The Self is not breakable. The essence is not going to break." You break only that which is breakable—the addictions and dependencies, the outside shells. In finding your real "I," you also find your uniqueness.

Discovering your "I" is not a form of selfishness. Rather, it is *self-reverence.* Finding yourself, you experience and revere the same pure "I" in all. In your aloneness, you are expanding your awareness of all-oneness. Now you know that in hurting others, you are hurting yourself, and that in helping others, you are helping yourself. Now what you see in you, you see in all living beings. When this state of "I" emerges, it becomes for you at the same time a merging—into the ocean of universal love and reverence for all life.

SEED-THOUGHTS FOR MEDITATION

Nirjara *is the way for me to drop, break, or shed conditions, addictions, and habits which bind me. I want to give myself room to grow. I want to free myself from limiting habits and reach my true height.*

What do I want? Why do I want? How much do I want? What I don't want I will not let into my life. What I do want is that which will help me grow and move toward my permanent reality.

I am I. I cannot be like somebody else. Wherever I go, I go with myself.

Religious vows are created from outside compulsion. Disciplines flow from inner self-awareness, from penetrating insights. They are like the banks of a river. If I keep these banks around me, I am freeing my energy to flow toward the ocean in a steady stream of awareness and love.

FACET TEN

The Nature of the Universse

WE are standing on the platform of human life. From here we have a choice. We can either go up with awareness or down with dependency. We have to decide between these two directions. It is our own decision. Nobody compels us to do this or that. There is no outside force which determines our course. We have to know that the deciding force resides within us.

Once we know this truth, we stop groping for things outside of us, and we start working from within. We determine what we want to do. If we have a longing to go up with awareness, this life becomes precious and meaningful to us. If we don't have this quest, life appears to be boring or meaningless.

Regardless of what one gives to this body, it is going to disintegrate. One day, it is going to go. If one doesn't use this body for moving toward higher awareness, then one will use it for temporary pleasure, gratification, or satisfaction. If one doesn't have an inner quest, then one can live for enjoying as much as one can, and doing whatever one wants. But in this case, there is no need to have a human body. To enjoy sex, to indulge in food, to accumulate things, to sleep a long time, to live in inertia, fear, aggression, one can have an animal form just as well as a human form. It does not matter.

Look at the animal kingdom. They are all doing the same thing. A bull can enjoy as much sexual pleasure as a human being. A bear can sleep for hours and hours with no one to disturb him. Compared to what an elephant can eat, what can a man eat? If you peer into the home of an ant colony, you can see their huge accumulation of food. Through all the seasons, they go on collecting. Think of the bees. They spend their lives in collection. There are human beings who do the same thing. They spend their whole time on earth collecting money, property, things, wealth, only to leave them behind when they depart. And sometimes the children who inherit this wealth call their parents fools and use the hard-earned money to finance their destructive habits and vices.

If this human life matters to you, you have to be very careful. You must know that this life can serve a great purpose. To serve this purpose, there is no better vehicle than this human body. You have to be very clear about what direction you want to take. That clarity of thinking will determine your course, your condition, your way. From this platform of human life, you will see that you have to move either upward or downward. The two are entirely different directions. They should not be mixed up.

To move upward, we need awareness. To go downward, we need attachment. What is attachment? It is clinging to things. Someone has mentioned that in attachment four things come: a little crying, a little sighing, a little lying, and a little dying. You cry because you want something. You sigh when you don't get it. To get it, you have to lie a little, and, ultimately, inside you die a little. From your own self you die, you separate. So when you notice these elements arising in you, say, "My goodness! Why am I crying? It is because of attachment!"

There is some confusion on this point. Many people ask, "Why should we run away from life? Should we not have joy? Can we not enjoy companionship with our friends? Is it not all right to have a good car, a house?" The teaching does not tell you not to enjoy life. On the contrary, it does tell you to enjoy your living. Only it objects to your crying, sighing, lying, and dying!

In fact, you can only enjoy all if you are not clinging or bound to anything. When you are not weighed down by dependency, you see things as they are. If something is here now, it will stay only as long as it has the nature to stay. So you enjoy, and when it goes, let it go. That is its nature—to go.

When you go to a florist, do you make a business deal with him? Do you agree to pay only if he can promise that the flowers will last for so many days? No, you select the best flowers, and they remain as long as they remain. That is all. When they wither, what do you do? Do you cry? Or do you accept, thinking, "For three days they have been beautifying the atmosphere, spreading a delightful fragrance"?

This is the approach of the enlightened person. You see as it is. You know that the flower is going to wither. At the same time, you are aware of the beauty and the fragrance of the flower. You have *double awareness.* You do not become sad and lose the joy of the moment. Because of the awareness of withering, you don't cry and say, "What will happen after three days?" The moment you see the flowers you are happy. You know that their living presence is offering joy to all, whether they are your friends or complete strangers. So you are not focusing on the withering at the moment that the flowers are in full bloom, although in your double awareness you know they will wither.

In this tenth reflection, the aspirant understands the nature of *loka*—this universe in which we all move. In this universe we all are permanent as well as transient. There are two standpoints. From the standpoint of essence, we are permanent. From the standpoint of form, we are transient.

As we grow, we see with double awareness two qualities: *dravya,* or substance, and *paryaya,* or modification. *Dravya* is essence and is by nature permanent. *Paryaya* is form, that which revolves or alters around the essence, and is by nature transient. We see in the same moment both the essence and form. We experience both the flower in bloom and its changing elements.

This deep awareness which comes from meditation makes you live in this moment of the present, not in the worry of tomorrow. What is to be gained by running to a palmist or astrologer and asking her to tell you how long you will live? If someone tells you you are going to live eighty years, what do you do? Perhaps you say, "Well, I have a long time to live," but are you happy? What do you do with the eighty years if they go in sickness, in the hospital, in distorted thinking, in bed? What if someone told you you have only one year to live? You would become anxious and say, "After one year, I am gone. What shall I do?"

You may know how long you will live, but do you know *how* to live? What are we to do with the few years we have? Are we here to vegetate? If we know how to live, one year can surpass one hundred years. It is not how many years we live which brings us happiness. *Joy is not counted with years; it is counted with moments.*

Can we learn the art of living in the present moment and get in touch with our *dravya,* our essence? We are always thinking of the future. We worry about the future. We don't live in the present. That is our problem.

There was a retired gentleman who used to be president of a large steel mill and who was a millionaire. He had no reason to worry about his bank account, but he used to complain and fret about the devaluation of the dollar. I asked him, "What is the matter? You don't have money?" He answered, "Oh yes, I do, but if the dollar goes on melting like snow, what will happen to me?" This kind of mind is completely distorted. The worry is so big that the millions appear as nothing to him. The person becomes frightened by his own fear.

There is really no fear except the fear you have created. Once fear takes root in your mind, it will take you in thousands of different directions. Those distorted mental creations which we call black magic are nothing but the products of fear. When you have a fear, there are people who know how to capitalize on it and manipulate you.

That is why Mahavir spoke directly to the initiates, saying, "Anything you do out of fear has no meaning. You have to reach that state in which you see what the whole world is. Then what you do, you do out of fearlessness." When you are not under the shadow of fear, then you are able to enjoy the moment. A person who is under fear is not going to enjoy life. For example, if a prisoner is told, "Tomorrow you will be hanged, so today eat as much as you want and go wherever you want to go," he will not be able to enjoy food or anything. He will be trembling at the prospect of tomorrow.

In the same way, fear does not allow you to be spiritual. Even to remember God out of fear is nothing but a kind of bribery; it is not spirituality. Spirituality is always aware; whatever you do, do it out of awareness.

How do you transcend fear? The only way is to know the world as it is, to know what you are, to know your relationship with the world. You are here for what? When you know your real nature, you will know why you are here. When you can discriminate between your essence and your transient nature, then you will be able to transcend fear.

In this *bhavana,* there are two reflections: *loka* and *aloka.* This galaxy, this cosmos, this universe is *loka.* Knowing its elements, you know what was once unknown to you. Knowing the unknown, you will be free from fear of the unknown. You will feel at home in this universe and move to your goal in fearlessness and conviction.

The constituents of *loka* are these six: *jiva,* soul; *ajiva,* matter; *dharma,* the law of motion; *adharma,* the law of rest; *akasha,* space; and *kala,* time. Space is the container of all the contained. What does it contain? Form. What is form? It is another container. Contained in form, like a bird in a cage, is *jiva,* conscious energy.

Loka is also a place in which two laws function, the law of motion and the law of rest. Owing to the existence of these two laws, the two energies called soul and matter are moving from place to place, alternating between movement and rest. Because of the functioning of these two laws, *loka* is that place where the atoms of matter compose and decompose. Matter is continually forming and unforming. Because this process occurs in a sequence, time can be perceived. The soul too, relatively speaking, is taking time to make its way out of its cage. Relative to the conditions or forms—physical, emotional, psychological—which surround it, a soul's journey can be measured in time. If there were no forms, a soul would be in its limitless nature. Then, from the height of this vantage point, time would not exist.

The opposite of *loka* is *aloka.* We can call it the void, because nothing exists here; it is only space without existence, without life.

At the frontier between *loka* and *aloka,* Enlightened Ones find their ultimate resting place, their height of consciousness. Until they reach this point, souls are in a process, on a journey, subject to certain limitations. *Moksha* is freedom, limitlessness. Once the soul drops all of its karmas, sheds every particle of matter encasing it, it finds uninterrupted peacefulness. There is no fight, no movement, no journey, no need. There is no desire to go anywhere because the soul has now reached a state in which it experiences life in completion, perfection, and desirelessness, which is fulfillment. *Jiva* dwells here in its own nature radiating its qualities of soothing peace and bliss, infinite love, and perfect knowledge.

The souls who reach this frontier are *Siddhas,* or Perfect Ones. Those who have freed themselves from all limitations and inner weaknesses come to rest here. From all religions, from all cultures, from all time periods, they ascend to this place where there is no duality, only unity. This ultimate quenching of the soul's quest is *moksha.*

When we take a look at *loka* from another perspective, we see that there are two aspects: the outer and the inner. The outer universe is the universe of fact. It is a constantly changing process. The forms it takes are a construction of ever-changing material elements. The inner universe is the universe of fantasy. It is composed of thoughts and emotions.

First let us see the outer universe as it is. Like the bits and pieces of a kaleidoscope, it is nothing but the combination and permutation of forms of matter ceaselessly building innumerable designs. Its main elements are earth, water, fire, and air. These elements combine and come apart, combine and come apart. According to the various stages of this process, the outer appearances are also constantly changing.

Mahavir used a vivid word for matter: *pudgala. Pud* means to fill and *gala* means to empty or dissolve. Our body is filling and dissolving every minute. Old cells are dropped and new cells replace them. The process of cell-building and cell-disintegration is constantly active. Twenty-four hours a day this process goes on, even while we are asleep.

When we understand the body's *pudgala* nature, we become aware of how to take care of it. We learn to empty it properly before we fill it up again. Yoga postures are practiced to eliminate toxins from the body. We exhale fully so as to discard all carbon dioxide from the body. To keep the body clean and healthy, we must know how to eliminate waste. Then we are ready to fill it with the proper nutrients in food and water, and with fresh air.

We see the body as a process. We understand the nature of its insentient energy. It is different from *jïva,* conscious energy. There is no reason to identify with it. There is no reason to praise or blame it. We see the body as it is.

The process of *pudgala* is true of our inner universe as well. Just as our cells are constantly changing, our emotions and thoughts are continually renewing themselves as well. Emotions and thoughts are fine forms of matter. They are the constructions of our inner *loka.* Thoughts are the bricks of the mind; emotions are the plaster cementing the bricks together.

You can transcend this process and see that whatever forms you create in your mind are capable of being dislodged, removed, or transmuted. Once you know this, you don't hold on to an old opinion of yourself or of any person. You are not the same now as you were a moment ago, a year ago, a lifetime of awarenesses ago. The old bitterness of the past can be dissolved within minutes. He or she whom you knew in one way may be a completely different person today.

There are examples of people who change the entire structure of their inner world when they catch a glimpse of themselves. Within minutes they transform their lives. How is this possible? The soul has tremendous power. Its light is more intense than the laser beam. In meditation, focus that light on a particular inner structure, and a miracle can happen. In a flash of insight, karmas can be dissolved. The cumulative effect of focusing your awareness on any undesirable element is to remove it once and for all and to lift a lifetime's burden.

You may ask why we call emotions and thoughts a fine form of matter. The soul or conscious energy is meant to flow in a steady stream toward the awareness of itself —as an immortal blissful energy of love and truth. It longs to experience universal consciousness and join the company of the *Siddhas.*

But from beginningless time, it has been in the company of matter. Its flow has been limited by certain kinds of particles which have been around it, acting as coverings. These particles of matter are *ajiva,* inanimate energy. They are the conditions in which the soul finds itself. As the soul perceives the outer universe through the senses and the inner world through the mind, it is continually influenced and conditioned by the presence of particles of matter. It is in what may be called a matter-dominated state, and it attracts additional karmic vibrations or particles. These karmic formations become what we call emotions and thoughts.

In this way, your inner universe becomes a complex

structure of biases, demands, expectations, projections. They are nothing but the accumulation of vibrations which have become crystallized as thought forms and emotional blocks. Their presence in you blocks the pure flow of sentient energy. If you allow yourself to be attracted or repelled, to act, react, and be acted upon, without checking the process, then your soul becomes laden with layers and layers of matter. They are like coats of armor obscuring your direct experience of Self.

When you become aware of your pure formless nature and stop identifying with matter—physical, mental, and emotional—you can stop attracting matter. But if you continue to be swayed to and fro, you will not be able to unburden your soul to let the steady, radiant, flickerless flame come out.

Once we know the construction of the universe, we realize that there is only one among the six substances which is aware—that is *jiva,* the Self. Time does not know anything. Space does not know anything. Matter is incapable of awareness. The laws of motion and rest are not aware. They are all inanimate. Truly, awareness pertains to the Self only. Our Self knows everything. When we know this, we are not confused. We focus on the inside universe which has the key to all the puzzles in our life.

Everybody has an inner universe. Look at your universe and ask, "What do I depend on? How can I depend on ever-changing change? What is this desire to hold on to things? Is it not ignorance? Am I not bumping up against mental walls, opinions, concepts, and expectations instead of being free in my universe? How can I hold on to that which is moving?"

Someone can stand in back of a train, chain his feet to the ground, and hold the train with his arms to stop it from going. He can use all his strength to keep it from moving. If he does, what will happen? He will be split. In the same way, you are split inside. You are clinging to things, to shadows, to transient elements, while life is passing by. You are putting yourself into a box by saying, "No, I want this to stay. It must not move. I want it to be permanent."

You are focusing on the wrong thing. You are trying to make the impermanent permanent instead of seeing that only the permanent is permanent. You have a fear that it will go away. Even if you deny the fear, how can you stop the change? There is no device in the world with which to stop it. That is the main point.

As soon as you try to stop someone or something from changing, you kill its nature. You block its life force. And when you have destroyed its nature, you no longer like it. Why? Because it is not natural, not spontaneous. The life inside departs, and the form starts to dry up and wither. Just like a corpse, its disintegrating form starts to give off an unbearable odor. And when you don't let someone else's nature flow, whose life stops flowing first? Your own.

So one has to stop jumping from point to point; one has to focus. Focus on what? On the limiting structures in one's inner universe. On one's addictions and their source, fear of change. Ask yourself, "How can I stop my fear, my anxiety? How can I stop expecting people to do as I want? How can I stop desiring to have a promise fulfilled?"

If you are truly aware, you will know that no one can promise you anything. From moment to moment, there are so many changes—in situations, in emotions, in the body chemistry. All one can do is to be open and receptive to the moment itself and say to oneself, "This is the moment!" Give yourself wholly to the moment, so that when conditions change and someone may not be able to keep his word, you retain the essence of the moment rather than the form it took. To depend on a promise is to invite sadness, for though it may be given in good faith, it may lose its validity with the changes which occur in time.

So let go of the moment and remember its essence. Realize, "My addiction to hold on to something or someone is my ignorance." It is difficult to accept one's own ignorant state of mind. If someone tells you that you don't know something, you become a little angry. "What do you think I am, a fool?" you ask. You do not want to hear the truth.

Addiction makes you angry, bitter, irritated, resentful. What happens is that you alienate the person to whom you are clinging. When he or she goes away, you become bitter. Why carry bitterness? Why sulk? There are those who recommend that you express your anger and show it openly. Instead, I say—vomit it; throw it out! The person you are crying for is gone; why continue to carry him around?

This can only come from inner understanding. As an initiate, you neither suppress nor depress. For you, it is a different direction. You cast out. You say to yourself, "I don't want to hold this unpleasant feeling; it will spoil the rest of the day, and I don't know when this day is going to come back." *Every precious day which goes from our life cannot be bought back by any means.* There is no currency in the world which can buy back the day which is going from our life. So if we cannot afford to buy the day, how can we afford to spoil it? This main awareness must permeate all parts of our consciousness. It must settle in.

Then, in the heat of anger, you will not be ready to

spoil your day. No matter how angry you are, you don't throw your ten-thousand-dollar ring from a moving train. You know its value, so you preserve it. In the same way, when you know the value of the day, you don't spoil it at any cost, not for any lover, not for any boss, not for any business, not for anyone who comes into your life. It is more precious than anything in the world. It is not going to come back.

This is called examining one's inner universe. You begin noticing any condition which makes you upset. You bring that condition before your inner eye and ask, "Why does this condition make me unhappy? Why does this habit spoil my day?" As you start discovering which conditions trigger an unbalanced state of mind, then you are using double awareness to watch the process.

So you see that you have become upset. That is the first awareness. Second, you watch yourself being upset. That is double awareness. In this way, you are both the observed and the observer. You are both the patient and the doctor. You are the patient because you are angry, and you are the doctor because you are curing. Your mind is the patient; your soul is the doctor.

Seeing with double awareness, you take each occasion as an experiment. You say to yourself, "This is my laboratory. Now I am going to find out why this disease has come." Each event provides you an opportunity to learn something more and to remove additional layers of *pudgala*—ossified mental or emotional blocks.

When we live within the confines of limited perception, we exist in a very small inner universe. We color the outer universe with these limitations and perceive it as a hindrance. When we break those inner confines, our universe expands with our awareness. We dance through the universe, connecting with each hand as we go. Communicating and sharing with sentient beings wherever we are, we perceive the universe of motion, rest, space, time, and matter as a means to help us celebrate reverence for life, to help us reveal our inner power.

You are *jiva,* a limitless, infinite soul! There is nothing to fight for, to compete for. Know what is your world and use it! From this platform of human life, you can see your present condition. Clear away the obstacles and forms cluttering your inner universe by becoming aware of their cause and their nature! Open the windows of your heart and mind and feel the spacious space inside! Meditate on this: "I am living, conscious energy. Let me melt away my inner walls of fear, greed, possessiveness, anger, and ignorance. I want to free myself from all the forms and live beyond."

Seed-Thoughts for Meditation

The constituents of this universe are soul, matter, motion, rest, space, and time. Of these six, only soul is aware. I have to reach that state in which I know these unknowns. Then what I do I will do out of fearlessness.

A flash of insight can lift a lifetime's burden.

When I know the value of the day, I won't spoil it at any cost.

Joy is not counted with years; it is counted with moments.

Soul is the doctor; mind is the patient. With double awareness I can heal my mind and make myself whole.

FACET ELEVEN

The Rare Occasion

THE mind is a ladder. If we are aware, it can help us move upward. If we are not aware, it can cause us to fall. This ladder has both potentialities—to be a help or to be a hazard. In its aware state, our mind is a beautiful instrument. It can receive and transmit truth. It can inspire and uplift us. But in its unrefined, unaware state, it works against us. It can trick us into thinking that what we want is right, when it may not be. We use it to rationalize that what we are doing is not wrong, when in fact it is.

When a person depends upon his intellect alone, he doesn't know whether he is rising or falling. He cannot tell because he does not rise above its particular bias. By allowing the intellect alone to judge, he manages to justify even an injustice. He will perceive as an ascent what is in reality a descent.

For example, a young man received his salary at the end of the week and started home with three hundred dollars in his pocket. By mistake he dropped his wallet. It landed on the sidewalk, but he did not notice. It happened that someone walking behind him saw the wallet fall. He picked it up, opened it, and saw the money. He was a good man and his first thought was to give it back. He pictured himself running up to the man, shaking him, and saying, "You silly young boy! Don't you know how to protect your money? Here it is!"

Then a new set of thoughts entered his mind. "For many days I have been out of a job," he thought, "and I have heard that 'God helps those who help themselves!' He helps us in many unseen ways. This must be one of the ways; otherwise, why should I have happened to be here when that man dropped his money? I did not have any theft in mind. I have not actually stolen anything. God has thrown a wallet before my eyes. It is a divine gift. How can I ignore it? It would be an insult to God! There is a reason behind everything, and this is a sign for me." In this way, he rationalized keeping the money and went home happily.

Waiting for him at home was his beautiful and serene wife. When he walked in the door, a whiskey bottle in hand, he announced to her, "Tonight we are going to celebrate!"

"How is that possible?" she asked. "We have no money."

"When you trust in God, He helps you," he explained. "The human mind cannot conceive of what God had in store for us today; He gave me three hundred dollars."

Again, she asked, "How did you get it?"

"A young man was going along and dropped his wallet," he told her. "So I picked it up. I did not do anything. It just fell into my path, a divine gift."

She spoke to him gently. "Don't you think that when he goes home smiling, full of hope and happiness because he has just received his week's pay, that someone like me is waiting for him just as I wait for you? Can you imagine his sorrow when he says, 'See, I have brought my pay!' and then finds out that his pockets are empty? Can you imagine his depression? What will he feel when he sees that a whole week's labor is lost? We can enjoy a dinner and a night of celebration, but what about the person who goes with hope and ends with hopelessness? Can you not think of that?"

The intellect is a sword with two edges. It can cut from either side. It can be used by a person for growth or it can be used to justify questionable things by saying that there is some divine hand behind it all. That is the kind of reasoning which has led people to justify even animal sacrifice as offerings to God. In the name of God, animals are killed. God does not eat their flesh, but the priests do while murmuring "Thanks." Thanks to whom? To the intellect which distorts, manipulates, and justifies even killing in the name of an unknown and unseen God.

Anything can be justified in that manner. Promiscuity is justified by calling it Tantra art. When you speak against it, you appear out of date, and people say you don't know what you are talking about. Others burn out their brain cells with drugs, yet justify it by saying, "I am in heaven, I see so many different colors." If you explain that it is merely hallucination, they laugh at you. If you tell them that what they see has no meaning, they say, "How do you know? You have not taken drugs." These are some of the ways the intellect can act as a ladder to take you downhill.

That is why the masters tell the initiates to purify their mind. It is raw; it is crude like oil. It needs to be refined. If you put crude oil in an airplane, what will happen? It will not take you up. Before it can be used, it has to go through the process of becoming gasoline. Once it has been refined, it can be used in a plane. You can depend on it. You are in the sky and you put your life in its hands. So refined gasoline is the right fuel with which to fly a plane.

In the same way, this mind, this intellect, in its crude

form can be dangerous. What we are learning here is how to refine it. It takes time. We don't want to discard it, abolish it, or blow it off. It is very precious. Imagine what power our mind has—it takes hundreds of people into the sky in a single jumbo jet. What is that which lifts the plane? Not the plane itself, but a human mind. If the human mind were not responsible for this feat, then the plane would not budge from the ground. Try throwing a stone into the air; it comes down. Even a feather does not stay in the sky. Here hundreds of thousands of tons are lifted into the sky for fourteen hours at a time! And we all trust it. The trust is based on what? Not on the inanimate plane, but on the human mind which created such a marvelous machine, and on another one that flies it.

Your life is more precious than any airplane. You cannot afford to waste it by stagnating, by keeping this intellect in a crude form. Engage yourself in refining it, and it will help you harness your energy, create beauty and harmony in your life, and move in the direction of evolution. How to refine the intellect? You take on a process of training, of awareness, of meditation. As you go on purifying, gross elements accumulated in the mind are dropped and it becomes clearer and clearer. That in you which is pure, subtle, and beautiful emerges. When you become subtle, even your thoughts become transparent, no longer heavy and crude. Thoughts no longer drive you in various directions. They begin to take you in the right direction.

For the initiates, this right direction, this refinement, this insight is called *bodhi. Bodhi* means to know, to be aware. It is the knowledge which comes from an inner opening, from inner experience. *Bodhi* has many more meanings. From this word is derived *Buddha,* meaning one who knows.

The eleventh *bhavana* is called *bodhidurlabha,* which means the rarity and difficulty of achieving such a deep knowledge. The path to Enlightenment takes time and energy to discover. In this reflection, the student marvels and rejoices at the fact that he or she has been able to seek out and walk this path. In fact, *bodhi* is such a rare and precious treasure that it has been compared to a unique radiant diamond. The lustrous diamond which Indian monarchs used to wear in their crowns was called the *Koh-i-nur* diamond. Such a diamond was not available to everyone; it was reserved only for special persons. In the same way, when we think of *bodhidurlabha,* we observe that inner awareness is a rare treasure that "common" people cannot afford. What is meant by "common"? It has nothing to do with post, position, wealth, or status. The common person is he or she who is living without inner richness.

How can you describe this inner treasure? Let us say that there comes a moment in your life, in your experience, when you realize that what dies is every *body,* not every *soul.* It may come from meditation, from hearing the words of the right teacher, from remaining in the company of the right person. Slowly it unfolds in you. You realize, "I am not a body. I am living *in* a body. I am unborn." So though you are born, you are unborn. It appears a little paradoxical. You might think, "How can I say I am unborn? I was born. I have a birth date." You know that that which has a birth certificate will have a death certificate. That is a fact. And it is horrifying to think that all of our efforts end in a graveyard. It is such a sad, tasteless thought.

So we go deeper. We go beyond intellectualization.

We begin to have the experience that something in us does not believe in death. If we truly believed in death, we would not get up in the morning. When we hear of somebody who has died, we feel a little sad, we inform someone else, and then we go on our way. Even though we hear of someone else's death, we do not think about our own death.

Why do we not think, "Death is coming. I had better take precaution"? When we sense danger coming, we take the necessary precaution. Is not death the biggest danger? And yet we enjoy life. Think for a while. Does it mean that we don't believe in death? Are we skeptics? Do we think it is only an illusion? If it were real to us, we would be serious about it, and yet we are not serious. That shows that we see, yet we don't believe in our seeing. We don't trust our eyes. Like a mirage, it is seen, but we know it is not water. Knowing that it is not water, we don't run after that mirage.

In the same way, we see death, and yet we are not afraid. There is a real meaning to this. The secret is this: the Inside Dweller *knows* that he has no death, because he has no birth. The Inside Dweller is unborn. Inside life is authentic. We realize, "What dies is the body, not me. The senses will die. I am not the senses, I am beyond them. I am using the senses as windows and taking care to keep them clean while I live in this house, the body." The Indweller does not identify with the house or with the windows. They are separate from the seer.

If the windows and the one who sees are one, then there will be no seeing, no seen, no process of seeing. So here we realize that when a person becomes old and closes the eyes, still he can see inside. The Indweller experiences what he or she has seen at another time.

When you experience this kind of knowledge, you don't say, "I am the possessor of knowledge." Instead, you say, "I *am* knowledge. Before, I was covered by ignorance. Now I am uncovering myself. I was hidden. Now I am coming out. I am removing the veils, the curtains until the reality of my Self is revealed." When you believe in you, you start experiencing inner richness. That gives you such a deep confidence that insights start coming and doubts drop away. Doubts which came from the outside stay outside; they don't belong in your inner world.

Before we begin to unfold our inner treasure of *bodhi,* we are covered with *mithyathva,* ignorance. Because of ignorance, we take one thing for another. Our main mistake is this: we take the body for the soul and the soul for the body. In this confusion, there is pain because of being unable to discriminate between the two. When something happens to the body, immediately we allow the soul to become identified with it. From this, our moods, fears, depressions, and projections begin.

Because of *mithyathva,* we do not see that the longing of the soul is an entirely different thing from the desire of the body. When these two are mixed up, then love is taken for lust, and lust is taken for love. We need one thing, but we take another thing instead. So we must ask ourselves, "What is my longing for soul companionship? What is the desire of my body to get gratification?"

We need love. It is the food of the soul; we cannot live without it. Love is not planning, it is not remembering. It exists only in the present moment. In love, there is no desire to hold, possess, or bind. To hold on to someone or something else is to disconnect from oneself. In disconnecting from yourself, you disconnect from the present moment, because your energy is used on the future. In this way, the experience of life, of love is slipping through your fingers. When you begin to see this very subtle point, you come to know that love has nothing to do with the past or the future.

Love is to just be. It means to be in communion. You can be in communion with any being that communicates and builds some kind of feeling and harmony with you. You can be in love with a plant, a child, an animal, a grandmother, a villager, a simpleton. It is possessing nothing, only being present in that moment, feeling and communicating with life in different forms.

In the same way, you experience this unconditional love with your own Self. You are in tune with yourself. When a person is in love, he does not hold anything back. He pours all his treasure without reserve. He does not say, "If I keep it, it will be useful one day." No, he says, "Here is the day, let me live it." You create this experience each day and turn it into your life style. In this way, you will no longer sadden your day with future thoughts and worries. Your living will be here and now with love.

The initiates are taught to live as brothers. The monks live together, yet they retain their individuality. The word "retain" usually implies that there is a plan behind what is being done. In this practice, individuality is retained without a plan or intention to retain it. How is this possible? It's a very subtle point; it is precisely because you don't have any intention to retain your individuality that you are able to retain it.

This approach is difficult to conceive, because you have been taught that you must make a plan, identify with something, attach to something. But here you don't have any tie; what you have is you! When you understand this, you separate from the past, you step away from the future, and you ask, "What does remain when I disconnect myself from everything? What remains is myself. What remains is my life. This is what is communicating in this moment." It is here and now, continually in communion.

This eleventh facet, *bodhidurlabha,* helps you eliminate the gross elements from your intellect. You make it so fine that it becomes your ally. You come to understand that you are nothing but soul. And the soul has no mission other than just to be in communion. From here let the idea of achievement drop.

We are all oriented to the idea of achievement. Many people ask, "What did you achieve in your life?" If you continue to ponder this question, you may conclude that you are a failure. You may think, "What did I achieve? Nothing. All my life is in vain." I have heard these same words from people of all walks of life. They say, "I feel I have been a failure. I wanted to be a doctor, but I failed in school. I wanted to be a lawyer, but I did not get the proper credits. I wanted to be an actress, but I did not get a good chance. I wanted to find a good partner in life, but they all cheated me." I have seen clerks who wanted to be managers, and managers who wanted to be owners. It reflects the way in which people live and act with the thought of failure.

What is achievement? In my college days, I witnessed the second richest and most powerful king in India, the Maharaj of Mysore, Krishnarajvadiar, turn into a heap of ashes on his funeral pyre. Afterward, I saw all the elephants, horses, and army return to the palace. He who had so many possessions, a huge palace, was lying alone in the wilderness, reduced to a handful of ash. Billions and billions of rupees, name and fame, what did it all mean? Is this achievement?

But this mind is not ready to understand. This mind is always making you unhappy, giving you the thought that you have not achieved anything. It mocks you. In this inner mockery, you are unhappy. No matter what you do during your day, when that thought comes, "What did you achieve?" all is in vain. The mind puts down even the good deeds you have done. It compares you to this person and to that. And this failure bites you, saddens you, weighs on you. You become so heavy that you don't derive any joy from life. And there will always be someone somewhere in the world who has more or who has done more than you.

So the master tells the initiate, "Your achievement is *bodhidurlabha.* Your achievement is to be aware of the real and the unreal, to be aware of your inner wealth living inside your outer garments." There is neither right nor wrong, only the real and the unreal. They have become confused. It is meaningless to blame anyone for this mistake; it is important only to see the way in which conditioning and unawareness have kept us from distinguishing between the two.

This allegory points out the confusion. One day truth and untruth both went to take a bath in the river. It was summer, so they took off their clothes and dived in. They were swimming happily until untruth got an idea. She came out from the river first and put on truth's dress. When truth came out and saw that her dress was gone, she said, "It is not good to go naked in society, so let me wear the dress which is left over." Since that day, the two have been moving in society and people don't know which is which because of their outer appearances.

See the reality rather than only the outside dress. Don't be deceived by appearance. See exactly who is wearing the dress. What we see with our eyes is deceptive because the real is inside. It can't be seen only with our eyes or heard with our ears or touched with our hands. It is beyond all the senses. It resides in our very central core. Because of its intangible presence, we can perceive the tangible world.

What you see is outside of you, but the real seer is inside. This soul is not born nor is it going to die. *When you realize this in your deep experience, this is your greatest achievement.* All other achievements are outer. They remain outside, becoming ashes on the cremation ground. But in this achievement, nothing leaves you, because you are your awareness.

That is why it is meaningful to meditate on the rarity of this occasion. We realize, "This rare insight, more rare than any sparkling gem, I have received into my heart. It is not going to go away from me. It is here and now, making me whole and complete. It is my inner divinity. That is why I can say I have achieved." Whenever you feel the lack of worldly achievement, remind yourself of this incomparable treasure, this precious inner wealth. Continue to remind yourself each day until you have completely convinced your mind.

That is your work—to purify your mind, your intellect, through and through. Once it is refined, it will be a useful ladder, a means by which to lift yourself up rather than a reason for you to fall down. When you ascend to the height, the clarity within, you will be ready to realize the last facet of reality: *dharma,* spiritual essence, inner truth.

Seed-Thoughts for Meditation

I do not possess knowledge; I am knowledge. Removing the veils, I am revealing myself.

When I confuse the desire of body with the longing of soul, I don't see what love is. Love is the nourishment of soul. It is to just be and not to possess. It is to be in communion.

Let me celebrate the unique moment when I realize that I am eternal, unborn, imperishable. When I experience this rare inner treasure, this will be my greatest achievement.

FACET TWELVE

The Nature of Our Nature

LIFE is an ocean in which the waves and ripples are constantly moving. There is not a moment in which they are still or steady. Continuously there is ebb and flow. In this ocean we too are moving along with the waves. Because of the ripples our minds are not steady.

When we are not certain about ourselves, there arises in us great confusion. We don't know what we need or where to go. We do not even know why we are here. Ultimately, the only thing which remains for us is to fill the empty days with trivial and meaningless activities. But such old, worn-out elements in our life must be thrown out like trash. Otherwise, we remain like children, creating make-believe and holding on to small toys. Our life remains on the surface, playing at fantasy instead of revealing the real depth of our being.

So we ask ourselves, "In this restlessness and unsteadiness, what is permanent?" The waves and ripples are not lasting; emotions and thought forms are ever-changing. Then the last step comes to the initiates—to come out of the tossing sea onto the island of *dharma,* your reality. *Dharma* has many meanings: reality, religion, truth, and nature.

* * *

The first meaning of *dharma* is reality. When you reach a deep experience of your reality, you are able to remain steady. If you do not reach that steady island, then you will always be in a state of action, reaction, and interaction, continually dealing with the senses, desires, emotions, and thoughts. There is no end to them! No sooner is one desire fulfilled than another desire arises, like the ripples in the ocean. As the tide draws one out, it sends another one in.

How many ripples are you willing to stand and count? How many times are you willing to be pushed and pulled by the waves? Think of your life. Do you recall ever having said to yourself, "If I fulfill this objective, I will be happy"? That may have been five years ago, and that objective may have been fulfilled, but still you are not happy. One desire has subsided, but another has emerged. This is the nature of the mind when it does not discriminate desires and demands for objects and pleasures.

How can you be contented unless you reach some steady place in your life? Your dharma *is that place.* The experience of the joy of being with yourself is greater than any other joy in the world. There is no other experience which can surpass this inner peace and tranquillity.

It is your desires which have not allowed you to reach that core, that center, that reality. That is why you may not know the joy of calmness you can experience in contentment. Desires constantly take you away from your core. Even when you sit in meditation, there are ripples disturbing you. You may tell yourself that meditation is boring or tiring. You may say, "I sat for two hours and got nothing but exhaustion." That is because you were not really meditating. You were wrestling with your mind. Where was there room for meditation?

When you reach that seat of consciousness where

nothing disturbs you, you become so calm. Before you reach it, you have to drop many, many things. As yet, you may not be ready to drop them. You hold on and think that someday they will be useful! That is why even in meditation you don't enjoy tranquillity, serenity, and peace. I tell you once you reach that center in you, you will not want to come out. To come out would be painful. You reach such a deep, deep peace that you do not want to move from that peace. No desire pesters you. Nothing bothers you. You are with yourself.

However, at that time, you recognize your body's needs when they arise. When your body needs some support, you give it what it truly needs. When it needs some rest, you give it rest. When it needs some nourishment, you give it food. The body is not a burden nor is it dependent on an addiction. What you do for it you do out of a recognition of its basic needs in order to maintain it as a fresh and healthy vehicle. Above all, your inner life is so full, so rich, that you feel you are getting nourishment and fulfillment from within.

When you reach that inner nourishment, you don't crave any temporary fulfillment which comes and goes. You see that temporary fulfillment never goes without leaving behind a scar; it carves out some small line of pain in you. Here in meditation there is no pain, no scar, only being in tune with reality. This is the first meaning of *dharma.*

Another meaning of *dharma* is religion. What is religion? It means to join or bind together. Separation is pain; union is peace. You have separated from your Higher Self; that is why you feel pain. Religion is a place inside where you are joining, uniting with your Higher

Self. Ultimately, one has to come together. There comes a time in a person's life when all outer attractions appear tasteless. When a person is in his eighties and you offer him what he may have liked at eighteen years of age, he says, "No, I don't want anything. It has had its own time. Now it is over. I want health and peace."

The word *dharma* in Sanskrit comes from *dhru,* meaning to hold or to lift. Anything which holds you or lifts you when you are about to fall into the valley is called *dharma.* That quality, that insight, that *dharma* is within us. Once we know it, we will not be able to fall. We must know this. Otherwise, friends, in each step there is danger; in each step there is the possibility of succumbing to so many temptations. There are not only physical and sensual temptations, but also the temptations of inside hatred, inside bitterness, inside anger, inside rejection.

Once you succumb to sorrow, depression, or bitterness, what happens? As you go on thinking, the emotions go on increasing. Bitterness becomes more and more bitter. Sadness becomes thicker and thicker. Observe your mind when you hold bitterness toward someone. Even when that person is gone, the bitterness remains. The person may not know how you feel toward him, but the bitterness rots inside you, besmears your mind, and pollutes your sweetness. In this way, life becomes heavy. You don't know where such negativity will lead you. It takes time to wash it out, to clean the mind. That is why in each step one has to be watchful and careful.

A person clinging to bitterness does not like himself. Because of this self-hatred, he sees others as his enemies and feels that the world is conspiring against him. Psychologically, these distortions are called projections. They all come because one is not watching oneself. It is easy to fall into hatred, bitterness, sorrow, negativity; it is difficult to lift oneself out.

Drug addiction comes from this kind of negativism. Some may say that taking drugs is for getting high; really that is self-deception. The person who takes drugs does not want to be with himself. He wants to forget himself and hide the truth from himself. Unfortunately, by taking drugs, the person is slowly destroying his own brain cells. Brain cells which are naturally active no longer function, and the person wallows in a kind of slow motion. When these cells are burned, the intelligence, awareness, and keenness of thinking cannot shine forth. The mechanism by which they come out has been destroyed.

In this *bhavana,* you have to watch what you are doing and remember to meditate constantly on your reality. Meditate on your inner unity and say, "I am I. Why should I worry about the opinions of other people? If I am not with myself, who will be? I will be I. That is all." All of the problems arise from not remembering the Self. It must become your habit day and night to remember it as you remember your own name. Your name is merely a tag, yet think how deeply this tag has gone. Even in sleep, you remember your name. If someone mentions it when you are asleep, you will open your eyes and say, "Hello!" If your name, which was given before you had a chance to approve of it, has gone so deep, why should not your own reality be as deep?

When one thing is taken for another, when a lie is taken for truth, when unreality is taken for reality, when the temporary is taken for the permanent, that is called *mithyathva,* or wrong belief. It is the most dangerous element in the path of a spiritual aspirant. It is this lack of clarity which causes us to take our name, which is temporary, to be permanent, and to think of our reality, which is permanent, as impermanent. So we have to be clear and know what is *dharma,* or the real, and what is *adharma,* or unreality.

Day and night, go on telling yourself over and over, "I am *Atma. So-hum.* I am That. Nothing else matters. Whether someone speaks in favor of me or against me, I don't care. I don't want to be restless, sad, or bitter. I want to be me." Hammer this into your consciousness! Then you will see how courageously you will be able to drop old habits, addictions, and needs. You will no longer be easily tempted or influenced.

Even when we constantly remember our reality and remain in tune with ourselves, we cannot remove temptations from the world. These things will remain; the difference is this: we don't identify with them. You may ask, "There are so many temptations. How can we remain in peace?" The answer lies in being vigilant. You have to know the nature of a thing before you take it in. You reserve the right to take it or leave it. Some one may offer you a sweet drink in a crystal glass. The fragrance promises sweetness to the tongue, but if you know that it has a drop of poison in it, you will not take it. In the same way, when you know that some idea or thing is not good for you, you make an inner decision not to take it into your consciousness.

Let us look at this process in more detail. We have four elements in our life—our body, mind, intelligence, and spirit. When these four are working together, life becomes meaningful. If we follow only one or two, there is some danger of imbalance. Suppose someone offers you an almond cake and you know that it has marijuana in it. The first reaction is the body's response. The eyes are attracted to the pleasing shape of the cake, the beautiful dish it is on. The nostrils enjoy the sweet fragrance. The tongue anticipates the delicious taste. Secondly, the mind wants it, thinking, "If I eat it, for two or three hours I will get some rest from this world and roam in the world of fantasy. I can enjoy a high." The mind wants that world of fantasy. That is why Disneyland is dear to children, and mythology is attractive to adults. The mind wants myths.

The third reaction comes from the intellect. If the intellect is pulled over to the side of body and mind, then you will in some way rationalize eating the cake. When the intellect, body, and mind join together, it is three against one. The soul is in slumber, and the majority rules. There is danger because you have not taken the consensus of all, and where there is no consensus there is no harmony.

When the mind gets light from the spirit, you act intelligently. You know how to wait. When you have awareness of *dharma,* then, though the body and mind want the cake, your intelligence tells you, "Yes, I hear you, body and mind. I know you want it, but once I get the habit, I will want it a second time. The chemicals will enter my bloodstream and create more and more need." Awareness of your inner reality guides you to make an intelligent choice, and the body and mind concur.

One must know the psychology of the vibrations of the body. Once you allow the chemicals in, you become a slave to them. They turn into desires and cravings. They enter slowly as humble guests, and you think, "Oh, it is only one or two drinks," but ultimately the drinks drink the whole human being. That is called alcoholism. Drugs also take over the whole system. There is a chemical influence in one's addiction to sex also. Even if the partner is full of negativities and a hindrance to one's growth, the person justifies the relationship because of the strong chemical influence. The person is not free from these physical and emotional bindings. The demand of chemicals is so strong that all spiritual ideas may go with the wind.

That is why there is so much pain, suffering, and misery in the world. That is why there are so many hospitals, so many mental institutions, so many drug addicts and alcoholics. They have missed a step. Ultimately, they end up being institutionalized because they cannot control themselves.

These habits have not come from birth. They come later on in life. They start with one weak moment, and enter the blood. If one wants to live long, happily, and healthily, one has to live very carefully.

No one is commanding you; you are commanding yourself. It is not somebody else's life; it is *your* life. There is no god controlling your life, it is you. If a person knows how to lift himself or herself, outside control is not necessary. No one has any power over us when we are with ourselves. In this way, we are all kings and queens.

Dharma bhavana means to take a stand in yourself. Know that you are responsible for yourself. If you don't take care of yourself, no one will. And no one has the power to rule your life unless you do that which is outside the law, out of harmony. So when your eyes, nostrils, and tongue want the cake, and your brain is ready to enjoy the fantasy, let your intellect align itself with your spirit and say, "No, it is not good for me. As long as I keep it out of my system, I have power. Once I accept it into my bloodstream, it has power over me."

In this way, *dharma* is the lifting element in you. There are moments in which you are on the rim, on the edge, of to do or not to do. In these subtle moments, who protects you? No friend is there. No outside element is there. It is you alone. You have to decide what you want to do. If you experience this conviction in your life, you will be strong in all circumstances. You will stop yourself from doing that which would hurt you or take you away from yourself. If you can save yourself in such moments, then you are permanently saved.

The third meaning of *dharma* is truth. When you first discover and then begin to live by inner truth, it becomes your measurement for everything. If an action fits with this truth, then you do it. If it does not, you reject it. It is not justifying; it is acting in accordance with your inner measuring rod. Truth becomes your permanent inner companion.

When you carry this within you, you don't have any fear, and when you are fearless, your energy flows naturally. Energy is dissipated by untruth. When you are false, you become unsteady, and your energy subsides. The body even begins to tremble; it is unnatural. With *dharma,* you move in the world with ease, without a hidden fear of being found out, because you live in truth. The whole world is available to you. The world is your home. Everyone you meet loves you. You have no need to hide. You are not seeing the world according to outside opinions and measurements. Your measurement is inside truth, inside authenticity.

The fourth meaning of *dharma* is nature. Everything has its own nature. The nature of candy is to be sweet. A thorn's nature is to prick. Salt is salty, and a rose's nature is to be fragrant. When you meditate, realize that everything is working in accordance with its own nature. The body, mind, and spirit are following their own *dharma.* Realize that there is no reason to blame or praise any form. See things as they are.

When you see things in this undistorted way, you can decide for yourself what you want. When you know the nature of people, you know how to deal with them. To be hurtful is a person's condition, not his nature. If someone seems to have a hurtful condition, you know that it is because of some previous experience, and he is trying to throw it off on someone outside of himself. But our nature is to be loving, compassionate, truthful, and uplifting. Knowing this, we will be patient with one another, and with ourselves. We have to know how to wait and give space before becoming involved in a new relationship or a new endeavor. First, allow the nature of the person, the place, or the thing to reveal itself to you.

Once a saint was staying near a river. He saw a scorpion fall in the water. Seeing that it would drown, he picked it up and put it on land. No sooner did he pick it up than the scorpion bit him. He felt the pain and covered his wound with a piece of cloth.

The scorpion went down to the river again and plunged in. Again it was drowning. "Silly scorpion," thought the monk. Compassion moved him again. There happened to be a man nearby who was watching this scene. He went over to the saint and asked, "What are you doing? Don't you have common sense? The scorpion bit you the first time, and still you let him bite you a second time?"

The monk smiled and said, "Even the scorpion at the moment of drowning is not ready to give up its nature to bite. How can I forget my nature of compassion? I can't be less than the scorpion. I must be I. This is my nature. Everything has its own nature."

This reflection brings you to your island of reality, your unifying strength, your inner measurement of truth, the innate nature of your nature. In this world where the waves are constantly moving, you do not have to be moving constantly with the ripples. If there is any steady place, that is the island of *dharma.* That is you. When you live on that island, you know, "Though turbulence may come, I shall not fall down. Though the winds of temptation may come, I shall hold my own. All else is temporary. Reality is here."

With this experience, you don't have bitterness or hatred for anyone. Praise and blame fall away from your life. You are careful about how you live in the world and about what you take into your life. You maintain your balance. What is the nature of your nature? To be loving, compassionate, truthful, blissful, and aware. To care, share, and dare—to care for life, to share with life, and to dare to achieve godhood, the height of your Self.

You know that everything in the universe will go away from you except this *dharma,* this truth. It is your everlasting companion. Experiencing this, you will never feel lonely. What comes and goes is the world, *samsara,* the ever-moving.

When feelings of loneliness come over you and you feel that there is nothingness, think instead, "There is somethingness; it is within me. It is *dharma.* It is the awakening of soul awareness." Feel it again and again until ultimately you never feel alone.

When you have this awareness, you are your own

teacher. The purpose of the outer teacher is to remind you of this: "Whether you are in the wilderness or in the city, on top of the mountain, in a forest or a cave, you are never alone. You are with your inner teacher, your *dharma,* your reality, your oneness."

Seed-Thoughts for Meditation

Let me stop being tossed and turned by the waves of unreality and step up onto my steady island, my dharma.

Separation is pain. Unity is peace. I separated from my Higher Self, that is why I feel pain. When I join my Self, nothing disturbs; I am in peace. This inside unity fulfills and nourishes.

No one is commanding my life. I am commanding myself. I have only to decide to be strong and not weak.

Whether someone speaks against me or for me, it does not matter. I am Atma. *On this island of my* dharma *I stand and keep my footing. All else is temporary; reality is here.*

Glossary of Sanskrit Terms

adharma—unreality
adharma—the law of rest
ajiva—matter
akasha—space
aloka—the void, space where neither matter nor soul exists
anitya—change, impermanence, transitoriness
anyatva—that which is other than Self
Arihanta, Arihante, Arihantanum—those who have conquered all inner weaknesses and have reached Self-Realization
asharana—unprotectedness
ashrava—inflow of vibrations
asuchi—the descending or decomposing
bahutva—manyness, multiplicity
bandha—binding
bhavana—reflection or meditation on different facets and aspects of reality
bodhi—deep inner experiential knowledge, Enlightenment, Self-Realization
bodhidurlabha—the rarity of finding the right path to Enlightenment
cattari—four
Dharma (in Pali, Dhammo, Dhammum)—reality, inner truth, that which lifts you and unites you to your Higher Self; the Teaching of Non-Violence, Peace, and Lovingkindness for all living beings
dharma—the law of motion

ekatva—oneness, aloneness
jiva—soul, consciousness
kala—time
karma—vibrations or particles of matter which bind, influence, and condition the soul until it uncovers itself and realizes its nature to be limitless, luminous, all-knowing, blissful energy
Kevali—Arihantanum or Omniscient Ones who gave us these insights and truths
loguttama, loguttamo—supreme, unsurpassed in the universe
loka—the universe
mangalum—auspiciousness, blessedness, blessings
mithyathva—wrong belief, unawareness, confusion
moksha—ultimate liberation, Self-Realization
nirjara—cleansing, breaking, shedding negative vibrations and conditions
nitya—changelessness, permanence, immortal essence
pannato—uttered by
pavajjami—I go to, I merge with
pudgala—that which fills and empties, matter
Sahu, Sahunam—saints, seekers
samsara—the cycle of birth and death, the ever-moving wheel of change
samvara—stoppage
sharana, sharanum—inner protection, refuge, strength
Siddha, Siddhe, Siddhanum—Perfect Souls who have reached *moksha*
suchi—the ascending, the spiritual, the pure
swa—the Self
swatva—Selfhood